POLYMER CLAY
MASTER CLASS

POLYMER CLAY
MASTER CLASS

Exploring Process, Technique, and
Collaboration with 11 Master Artists

JUDY BELCHER & TAMARA HONAMAN

POTTER
CRAFT

NEW YORK

DEDICATION

My greatest collaboration is with my ever-patient husband, Greg: our children, Maria and Max, to whom I dedicate this book. And to Tam, for our special friendship and her great command of words.
—Judy

Dedication and heartfelt thanks to Rich, my husband, and our boys, Kevin and Ryan, for their never-ending love and support. And to Judy, for her energy, friendship, and for inviting me to the party.
—Tammy

Copyright © 2012 by Judith S. Belcher and Tamara L. Honaman
All rights reserved.
Published in the United States by Potter Craft, an imprint of the Crown Publishing Group, a division of Random House, Inc., New York.
www.pottercraft.com
www.crownpublishing.com
POTTER CRAFT and colophon is a registered trademark of Random House, Inc.
Library of Congress Cataloging-in-Publication Data
Belcher, Judy.
        Polymer clay master class : exploring process, technique, and collaboration with 11 master artists
/ Judy Belcher and Tamara Honaman.
        p. cm.
1. Polymer clay craft. I. Honaman, Tamara. II. Title.
    TT297.B454 2012
                    2012011921

ISBN 978-0-8230-2667-8
eISBN 978-0-307-96575-2
Printed in China
Design by La Tricia Watford
Photography, unless otherwise specified, by Richard K. Honaman Jr.
Cover design by La Tricia Watford
Cover photography by Richard K. Honaman Jr.

10 9 8 7 6 5 4 3 2 1

First Edition

TITLE PAGE: Lindly Haunani and Leslie Blackford, *Mystery Masks*, 2010; polymer, acrylic, oil, alcohol inks, and barn wood; 20 x 10 x 3 inches (51 x 25.5 x 7.5cm). Photograph by Leslie Blackford

"Many years ago I played in Leslie's studio as part of a group effort to help jump-start a series of masks she was making for a show. So when I approached her about doing something similar as an exchange/collaborative piece for the Synergy2 exhibit, I was thrilled when she agreed. The title of this piece is *Mystery Masks*, since it was a mystery how the piece would come together. The process of working with Leslie inspired me to try a looser, more three-dimensional style."
—Lindly

OPPOSITE: Dayle Doroshow, Sarah Shriver, and Robert Dancik, *Collaboration!*, 2011; polymer, copper, and found objects; 4½ x 4 inches (11 x 10cm). Photograph by Richard K. Honaman Jr.

"On my morning walk along the ocean, I noticed various bits and bobs in the sand. I knew Robert used found objects in his artwork, so I decided to collect a few for him. He immediately suggested we collaborate. A couple mornings later, I discovered a beautiful piece sitting on my work desk along with a note asking me to add something. Sarah and I had made several small beads that we were not going to use for our final necklaces. One went perfectly at the bottom of Robert's piece."
—Dayle

ACKNOWLEDGMENTS

Our deepest appreciation goes to each of the artists who participated in this adventure; their ability to share, explore, and trust humbles us. Great thanks to Rich Honaman for the hard work and long days he put in to make the images fantastic, and for his ability to whip up a mean cocktail. Jeff Dever's belief in us and the support he offered, both during the planning of the book and during our week's exploration, were critical to the success of this experiment. His help during our time together on the Outer Banks—spurring conversations, stirring collaborations, and providing great topics for discussions at dinner—proved invaluable and added so much to the experience and printed word. All of us felt spoiled by the never-ending supply of delectable meals and snacks that Jim Glass provided. What a delightful surprise it was for the artists to open box after box from companies who generously donated polymer, supplies, and tools for the artists to use; grateful thanks to Polyform Products; Van Aken International; Staedtler; Viva Decor; Ranger Industries, Inc.; and Fire Mountain Gems and Beads. As we embarked on this journey, Joy Aquilino understood our vision and gave us wonderful guidance and support. Alison Hagge, our project editor, took our manuscript and crafted a page-turning story that brings you into the house with us. Betty Wong, Caitlin Harpin, and La Tricia Watford from Random House all helped to turn it into a beautiful book.

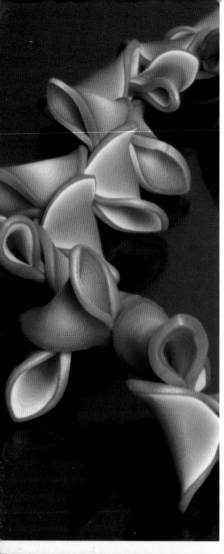

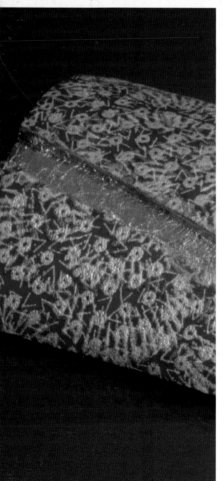

CONTENTS

FOREWORD BY JEFF DEVER

Collaborations between artists may be one of the most powerful catalysts to revitalize, refocus, and redirect one's work—to infuse your vision with a jolt of energy. In one week at the beach, eleven talented artists created five spectacular collaborative projects—testaments to the synergies born out of this bouillabaisse of personalities, aesthetics, and temperaments. Some of these artists are seasoned collaborators, well versed in the dance of self-expression and negotiated compromise; others were newbies, collaborative virgins on an artistic quest.

As our artists discovered, collaboration is not a one-size-fits-all journey—there is no road map, and no two paths are alike. To work successfully with another artist requires honesty, communication, artistic self-confidence, and, most of all, trust. One should be neither a diva nor a doormat, and embrace an open mind and heart. Every collaborator receives directly in proportion to what they invest, and commitment to the process is key. Whether the path is smooth as glass or strewn with pitfalls, no artist remains unchanged. We discovered that all who enter will grow; even if their work appears unchanged, they will forever be informed by the journey. Ultimately, the test is not the final piece of work but our evolution as artists, born of collaboration.

OPPOSITE: Leslie Blackford, *Carnies*, 2011; polymer and ephemera; dimensions variable. Photograph by Richard K. Honaman Jr.

Leslie arrived at the beach with a special treasure for each of us: our own personal carnie necklace. She knew enough about each of us to make a character that touched on a bit of truth. Clockwise from twelve o'clock: Lindly/fortune-teller, Seth/strongman, Jim/Pagliacci (sad opera clown), Dayle/ballerina, Julie/acrobat, Leslie/voodoo kitty, Tammy/cat woman, Wendy/octopus girl, Judy/mime, Sarah/gypsy, Cynthia/superwoman, Jeff/magician, Rich/ringmaster, Robert/swordswallower, and Sandra/trapeze artist.

INTRODUCTION

Most artists work in isolation in their studio. Historically, there is near reverence for the image of the solitary individual, lonely and suffering. Yet most artists desire to have creative discussions with others. That is why retreats and workshops are so popular—it's why we join organizations, participate with online groups, and follow each others' blogs. Collaborations, "bees," and workshops in the creative arts not only provide a mixture of fun and friendship, they also offer the perfect setting for learning.

As longtime friends and colleagues, we have always been fascinated by the interplay of artists at work. Having mulled over these ideas for years, we were delighted when the specific plan for this book finally hatched: *Polymer Clay Master Class* investigates the creative process of eleven polymer artists, each of whom was carefully chosen because she or he has a unique style as well as a keen eye that is able to discern what is relevant and exploratory in polymer today. We wanted to see what would happen if we paired up these artists, strong individuals with articulated aesthetics and refined working methods; challenged each team to create a collaborative work; provided lovely shelter, hearty sustenance, and stimulating conversation; but—*oh yeah*—gave them a firm deadline. Would creative synapses fire, unanticipated alliances form, and exciting collaborations ensue, or were we setting ourselves up to fail, to jeopardize some of our most cherished longtime contacts in the polymer community?

We decided to find out, and so we invited these artists to gather for a weeklong collaborative journey at the Outer Banks of North Carolina. The lovely beach home was the perfect backdrop, providing a warm and inviting shelter from the storms that were brewing on the ocean that week. Meanwhile, inside, intense investigation (along with fresh coffee) was brewing—as each of these artists presented ideas, listened to counter ideas, discovered common ground, respected differences, and otherwise established the requisite trust necessary for fruitful collaborations to emerge.

RIGHT: This magnificent home on the Outer Banks of North Carolina provided an off-season retreat for artists who agreed to come together to push the limits of their creativity. **OPPOSITE:** The last day of our adventure! The wind was blowing, and we were distracted by the pod of twenty dolphins that happened by that morning, but were feeling happy about all we accomplished. Front row (left to right): Rich Honaman, Tammy Honaman, Dayle Doroshow, Wendy Wallin Malinow, Leslie Blackford, Cynthia Tinapple, Julie Picarello, Seth Saverick, Sandra McCaw, Judy Belcher, and Lindly Haunani. Back row (left to right): Jeff Dever, Robert Dancik, Jim Glass, and Sarah Shriver.

It was captivating to watch these projects unfold. A few teams worked quickly with loud whoops and lightning-fast hands; some labored quietly and methodically, working and reworking components until they were satisfied with the outcome. Some teams melded their styles so completely that the final work is unrecognizable as having either individual's apparent style; others blended their processes or techniques to form pieces that on some projects were quite unexpected and on others made it obvious as to who had contributed what.

The pages that follow offer a front-row seat to this dramatic interlude. We have organized this book into five lessons—each of which encapsulates the theme that emerged for that particular team. Within each lesson, first, the team presents an overview of the challenges they faced while working together. Immediately following, lavish showcase sections allow the artists to formally introduce themselves and their work. Next, each artist shares a project, providing not only an in-depth exploration of his or her process, but also a unique, hands-on opportunity for you to try out a fabulous array of techniques. Each lesson ends with a detailed account of the team's collaborative odyssey—an honest (sometimes joyful, sometimes not) narrative that documents their intellectual, spiritual, and creative quest. They share stories about their process and—through their willingness to remain open to the spirit of collaboration—move in new and interesting directions.

This book is meant to be a master class in creating with polymer. As such, we hope that it inspires your own creative explorations and encourages you to seek out and embark on your own collaborative adventures. Whether you are learning how to build a career or have chosen polymer as a fun hobby, what you create is often intensely personal. Allowing someone else into that world can be uncomfortable at times, but it can also be exhilarating, providing just the right spark to ignite in you a desire to find your own unique voice. This life-changing experience has been a catalyst for new directions for many of us. Follow our journey; then take your own leap of faith. It is sure to be an adventure!

PARTICIPATING ARTISTS

Judy Belcher wore two hats for this project. You can read about her on page 158, along with Tam, her coauthor.

Leslie Blackford, a self-taught artist, is known for her ability to express raw emotion in her work. She allows her feelings to fly out of her fingertips and become art. This process is as natural to her as breathing. Her work can be found in galleries around the country and in permanent museum collections. Leslie teaches nationally and internationally, but her home and studio are in Kentucky.
Leslie Blackford, necklace of carnies from the *Damn Everything but the Circus* series, 2011; polymer and leather; talisman: 2 x 3½ inches (5 x 9cm); cord: 28 inches (71cm). Photograph by Todd Hodges

Robert Dancik holds a master's degree in sculpture and a BA in fine arts and has been an artist/teacher for more than thirty years. Author of *Amulets and Talismans: Simple Techniques for Creating Meaningful Jewelry*, he has exhibited his jewelry and sculpture in museums and galleries in the United States, Europe, and Japan. The originator of Faux Bone, Robert lives in Oxford, Connecticut, where he is an avid cook and collector of toys, maps, and compasses.
Robert Dancik, *Just Off North*, 2008; polymer, sterling silver, carnelian, hematite, amber, 14K gold; pendant: 3½ x 1⅜ inches (9 x 3.5cm); chain: 35 inches (88.5cm). Photograph by Douglas Foulke

Dayle Doroshow studied traditional ceramics in New York City and is now a mixed media/polymer artist and owner of the design studio Zingaro, Stamp of Distinction. She lives in Northern California, a place of natural beauty with an active and supportive artist community. Her art is frequently featured in West Coast art shows, galleries across the country, and in books. Dayle's passion is teaching, and she runs frequent workshops in the United States, Canada, and France.
Dayle Doroshow, *Portrait #1*, 2011; polymer, color copy, and black/white transfers collaged and layered on a coconut wood bezel; 2¼ x 2¼ inches (5.5 x 5.5cm). Photograph by Dayle Doroshow

Lindly Haunani has more than twenty years of experience as a polymer workshop leader. She is one of the founding members of the International Polymer Clay Association, coauthor of *Polymer Clay Color Inspirations* and *Artists at Work: Polymer Clay Comes of Age*, and the star of several how-to videos. Her work is part of the permanent collections of museums throughout the United States. She lives in Maryland and fantasizes about being a food stylist, stand-up comic, or fabric designer.
Lindly Haunani, *Green Petal Earrings*, 2008; polymer and niobium; 2½ x ½ x ½ inches (6.5 x 1.3 x 1.3cm). Photograph by Hap Sakwa

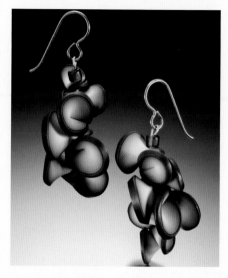

Wendy Wallin Malinow has always lived in Portland, Oregon, and grew up in a family of artists, which naturally led to a fine arts education in drawing and painting. In addition to illustrating sixteen books and many more gift/ad campaigns, she shows in several galleries and has work in four permanent museum collections. Wendy's mix of polymer and precious metals forms complex layers of meaning.
Wendy Wallin Malinow, *Woodland Rooted Man Shaker*, 2011; polymer, garnets, and glitter; 10 x 3 x 2 inches (25.5 x 7.5 x 5cm). Photograph by Courtney Frisse

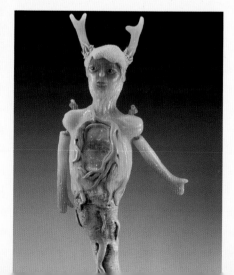

Sandra McCaw strives to lead a quiet, simple life in her home and studio in Massachusetts. With a museum-school education in illustration and photography, she is now acknowledged internationally as an innovator and leading polymer artist and teacher. Her jewelry has been exhibited throughout the United States and Japan, has been extensively published, and is represented in the permanent collections of major museums. Sandra McCaw, *Untitled*, 2008; polymer, 23K gold leaf, and gold-filled wire; 3½ x ¾ inches (9 x 2cm). Photograph by Hap Sakwa

Julie Picarello has a background in the computer industry, where for more than twenty years she has designed integrated circuits. She is the author of *Patterns in Polymer: Imprint and Accent Bead Techniques*. Her teaching has taken her to many venues and major shows throughout the United States and in Europe. Julie's home and Yellow House Studio are in the Northern California foothills. Julie Picarello, *Winged Turquoise*, 2008 (above right); imprint *mokume* polymer, polymer chips, handmade sterling findings, and miniature train parts; 6 x 18 inches (15 x 45.5cm). Photograph by Julie Picarello

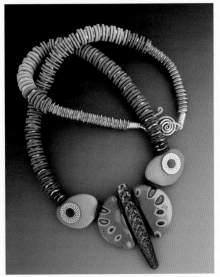

Seth Lee Savarick has had careers as a professional dancer, food stylist, graphic artist, and now as a studio artist and jeweler. He has taught art and design courses at the Parsons School of Design, the Corcoran School of Art, and the Maryland Institute College of Art. He has contributed to books and magazines and helped organize several international conferences. Seth sells his work through art galleries and boutiques in his current home of Los Angeles. Seth Lee Savarick, *Swashes Inro*, 2004; polymer, acrylic paint, liquid polymer, 18K gold powder, acrylic medium, and silk cord; inro: 5 x 3 x ¾ inches (12.5 x 7.5 x 2cm); cord: 24 inches (61cm). Photograph by Robert Diamante

Sarah Shriver is an internationally acclaimed polymer artist who generously shares her secrets at teaching engagements around the world. With a degree in fine arts, she has been working full-time from her home studio in San Rafael, California, for more than two decades, producing ever more magnificent designs, incorporating new techniques, and evolving the medium. Sarah is recognized as a pioneer and master of her craft. Sarah Shriver, *Bug Necklace*, 2008; polymer, glass beads, and brass beads; 1 x 32 x ½ inches (2.5 x 81 x 1.3cm). Photograph by George Post

Cynthia Tinapple of Worthington, Ohio, is the author of *Polymer Clay Daily* (http://polymerclaydaily.com), a blog that takes a highly curated approach to showcasing the best polymer art online. The site has a large, loyal audience and has helped build the polymer community worldwide and move it forward. Cynthia Tinapple and Blair Davis, *Penny Quilt*, 2010; polymer and walnut; 4 x 10 x 10 inches (10 x 25.5 x 25.5cm). Photograph by Blair Davis and Cynthia Tinapple

POLYMER BASICS

Polymer is a man-made modeling material that remains soft and malleable until it is cured. As evidenced in this book, it is a versatile art medium; it can be sculpted, carved, caned, molded, and so much more. Polymer is readily available in art supply stores and through catalog and Internet outlets. Each brand has different working characteristics, baking temperatures, and is produced in a wide range of colors that can be mixed to create your own custom palette. The brands of polymer featured in this book are those favored by the individual artists, but should your favorite be different, the techniques will turn out just as well; we advise you to experiment with all the brands.

Conditioning

Polymer must be conditioned before you can work with it. Conditioning it ensures that the ingredients are distributed evenly throughout and the end result is strong when cured. To condition polymer, slice the block into sections, and then twist each section with your hands; or if the brand is particularly stiff, use a pasta machine to roll and flatten each slice on sequentially thinner settings; then fold and roll some more until the polymer is soft and pliable. Take care to not trap air in the polymer; this can occur if it is too soft and sticky or if you don't roll it through the pasta machine with the fold side against the rollers.

"Conditioning creates an even distribution of all solid and liquid ingredients for ultimate effectiveness. Like a can of paint that has been sitting idly, a block of polymer clay contains solids that have separated from some of the liquids. Conditioning polymer clay serves the same purpose as shaking a can of paint—it brings it all back into suspension."
—Tony Aquino, Technical Director, Van Aken International (makers of Kato Polyclay)

Curing

The curing process is what hardens polymer. Each manufacturer recommends a time and temperature best suited to their brand; be sure to read the instructions offered on the packaging. Cure in a polymer-dedicated convection, conventional, or toaster oven. If curing in your home oven, place items in a roasting bag (used for turkeys or chickens)

so any released fumes are trapped in the bag. Always use an oven thermometer and check it often to ensure that the oven temperature remains consistent during the curing process.

"I'm not always good about checking my oven thermometer, but changes in the temperature of my studio or even the weather outside can sometimes affect the oven I use—so it's a good idea to leave a mercury thermometer in the oven and check it each time you cure."
—Leslie

Storing

Storing polymer in a cool area away from direct sunlight is important because direct sun and temperatures above 90°F (32°C) will begin the curing process and make the polymer unusable. Once the package is open, store any unused polymer in waxed paper, plastic wrap, or uncoated deli paper; or in a container. Do not use a container made from polystyrene-type plastic (recycling number 6), as it will react with the polymer and make some of it unusable.

"I keep my canes wrapped in waxed paper, in a dark closet."
—Sarah

"I try to keep pieces in progress dust free, and I also keep all mixed polymer in plastic, divided boxes. My studio, in a perfect world, would be more organized, but as much as I try, my big tables always have—at most!—about a twenty-four-inch square of uncluttered working space. I tell myself, maybe, that's just the environment that I need to work and design effectively."
—Wendy

Leaching

Polymer is leached in order to remove some of the plasticizer, stiffen the material, and achieve a desired consistency. To leach the polymer, sandwich conditioned sheets between clean, absorbent paper—like plain white copy paper—and weight it with a heavy book. Check the polymer to ensure that it is still pliable.

"The purpose of the plasticizer is to allow the polymer clay to remain workable and pliable and the baked piece to maintain some flexibility, strength, and durability. If too much plasticizer is taken out of the polymer clay, the artist would be able to tell, as the polymer clay will

be dry, crumbly, and difficult to manipulate—the extreme opposite of being too soft. Removing some of the plasticizer should have very little effect on the properties of the final baked piece."
—Iris Weiss, Education Manager, Polyform Products

Saving Scrap Polymer

When working on polymer projects it is inevitable that you will generate scraps, but these have many uses, so save them as you go. Scrap polymer can be used to make another color less intense, to form the core of a bead, or to make a mold.

To eliminate any air that might be trapped in scrap polymer, cut it into manageable piles and then thoroughly condition it—gently stretching the polymer between each pass through the pasta machine. This breaks the surface of the polymer where a pocket of air lies just below.

"As I work on different projects, I separate my scrap into color families to use in future projects; I am sometimes overrun with bags of color spanning the rainbow. When I am stuck with a particular design dilemma, I use the 'thinking time' to condition and sheet the scrap from the bags."
—Judy

Choosing a Finish

Consider the design of the piece when making decisions about the finish you choose. Uncured polymer is receptive to all sorts of textures: 60-grit sandpaper, textured wallpaper samples, and fabric or mesh screen, to name a few. After curing, you can leave the surface matte or buff it to a high shine. Buffing on a piece of denim will yield a subtle shine. To achieve a high shine, start sanding the surface with wet/dry sandpaper and water, working from 400- to 1000-grit, and then progressing to a motorized buffing machine fitted with a dry, unstitched muslin wheel.

"There are no oven fairies—what you put in the oven is exactly what comes out. Take the time to completely smooth the surface of the piece before you cure it. This simple process will greatly reduce the amount of time and effort required to sand and buff the piece to a high shine."
—Judy

| WHAT TO CALL IT? BY RACHEL CARREN |

From its beginnings, there have been questions about what to call this modern, synthetic modeling compound. Before 1990, both artists and publications describe the material using a brand name, such as Fimo or Polyform, with a modifier such as "modeling compound." Then, in 1991, with the publication of Nan Roche's *The New Clay* the descriptor "polymer clay" began to be used widely. Roche and her publisher, Seymore Bress, specifically devised the term as a reference to how the material is worked and its chemical properties. During the past twenty-plus years, the use and range of polymer art

has evolved significantly. Polymer art is now included in the collections of major American museums, and artists who work with it routinely exhibit at premier shows. The term *polymer clay* has become puzzling.

For museums and galleries, calling it "polymer" eliminates internal and public confusion over classifications; polymer art is not part of the ceramics collection. From a utilitarian point of view, the use of the material has become increasingly diverse so that many of the claylike qualities are secondary to what artists do with it. The term *clay* also leads to uncertainty in the retail market.

Customers who hear the word *clay* often assume that an item is heavy and fragile, neither of which is true with polymer.

As polymer art moves forward in time, the term *polymer clay* is unlikely to be abandoned, but the single word—*polymer*—can be embraced as a basic description of this material. Whatever one calls it, the material always requires a bit of explanation to the uninitiated, and the question of identification is apt to be refined further as plastics become more prevalent materials for artists.

POLYMER TOOLBOX

The Polymer Toolbox is a general assembly of tools to have on hand in addition to the items listed in the materials list in each project. This includes the following:

Pasta Machine

Many brands of pasta machines are available, each with its own numbering system. The projects in this book offer a guideline on thickness rather than a number—thick, medium-thick, medium-thin, and thin. Determine the appropriate setting for your pasta machine as you work through the projects.

Roller

A roller can compress layers of a cane and otherwise perform tasks not possible with a pasta machine. An acrylic brayer, acrylic rod, and knitting needle will suit your needs no matter what rolling you need to do.

Blades

It is advisable to have many types of blades on hand, as each has a benefit depending on the type of cutting you are doing. The types available are: stiff (for slicing through blocks of clay); flexible (for cutting on a curve or for creating curved cuts); tissue (for slicing canes or thin cuts); wavy (for creating ridged or waffle cuts); and craft (for maneuvering in tight spaces). All must be handled with care.

Work Surface

How you choose your work surface depends on personal preference and what you have available. Here is an assortment of ideas: safety glass, Plexiglas, self-healing mat, and large, smooth ceramic tile.

Portable Work Surface

Using a portable surface makes it easy to move a piece from your work surface to another location without disturbing it. Options for this include nonstick Teflon sheets, small ceramic tiles, plain or deli paper, fabric, and textured paper.

Baking Surface

Once you commit to curing polymer on a tray, that tray becomes dedicated to polymer—forever. Consider using standard baking sheets and ceramic tiles. Using cardstock as an additional baking surface makes your work portable from studio to oven.

Baking Needs

Some designs require support during curing so they don't collapse. Fiberfill, cornstarch, and baking powder all work well for this task.

Oven

You can use a conventional, convection, or toaster oven when curing polymer. Use a thermometer so you are sure that the temperature is accurate and constant at all times.

"I often tell my students that you really only need four tools to work with polymer: a large white work surface, a sharp cutting blade, a good pasta machine, and—most important—a magical sense of possibility. It's funny that I have eight running feet of five-foot-high drawers full of tools!"

—Lindly

Tools for working in polymer include a pasta machine, variously sized acrylic rods, an acrylic brayer, various blades (left to right: cheese knife, wavy blade, flexible blade, tissue blade, two stiff blades, and a craft knife), various work surfaces (left to right: Plexiglas, ceramic tile, self-healing mat, nonstick sheet), and an oven thermometer.

SKINNER BLEND TECHNIQUES

Judith Skinner developed and shared the wonderful technique that bears her name—the Skinner Blend—to easily create color gradients in polymer using a pasta machine. Polymer artists will be forever in her debt for providing a simple way to give depth and visual complexity to their work. Each of the artists in this book who makes use of the Skinner Blend embraces the technique and builds upon it to suit his or her work. What follows is an explanation of the concept as well as a few variations of the Skinner Blend in practice.

Judith Skinner, *Untitled*, 2005; polymer, pearls, and copper wire; 3 x 24 inches (7.5 x 61cm). Photograph by Steve Payne

Shortly after developing the technique and sharing it on the Internet, Judith attended Ravensdale—a large polymer teaching conference—where everyone in the room was already making her blends. Kathleen Dustin and Nan Roche insisted the technique be given a name, and so it was anointed the "Skinner Blend."

The Concept by Judy Belcher

One of the most-asked questions I get when teaching is, why does a Skinner Blend work? There isn't a simple verbal answer, as it combines mathematics, color theory, and a bit of Judith's magic. Yet, when presented visually, this concept is easy to understand.

In the demonstration here, each section—made of a different proportion of the two colors—is blended thoroughly. When each section is laid in order, side by side, you will see the gradual blending that occurs within a Skinner Blend sheet.

1. Choose two colors of polymer and condition them thoroughly. Roll them out on the thickest setting of the pasta machine. Cut each color into a 3 x 4–inch (7.6 x 10cm) rectangle.

2. Cut each rectangle in half diagonally. Stack the resulting triangles on top of each other, matching the colors. Re-form the rectangle by joining the butt edges of the seam of the triangles along the diagonal edge.

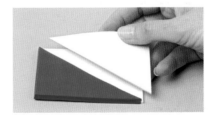

3. Using a ruler, measure and mark the polymer every ½ inch (13mm) to form 8 equal segments along the length of the rectangle. Cut each segment apart.

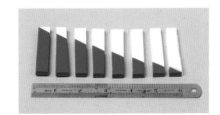

4. Thoroughly blend each separate segment using the pasta machine. Fold and roll each segment, making sure that the fold is placed against the roller, so you will not trap air in the polymer. The final image here shows each blended section and the two original colors.

TIP: Blending on a thinner setting makes quick work of this process.

Two-Color Skinner Blend by Lindly Haunani

1. Choose two colors of polymer and condition them thoroughly. Roll out the polymer on the thickest setting of the pasta machine. Cut each color into a square. Cut each square in half diagonally. Stack the resulting triangles, matching the colors. Re-form the triangles into a rectangle by offsetting them slightly along the diagonal edge and trimming the extending points. Keep the original colors pure along the edge. Gently press the seams.

2. With your pasta machine at the thickest setting, align the rectangular sheet to the rollers so that both colors are touching it. Roll the sheet through once to make sure the triangles don't separate.

3. Fold the resultant sheet in half, making sure that the two edges of the same color meet. The most critical part of the technique is how the polymer is folded and rolled through the pasta machine. After the initial roll through the machine, lay the polymer on your work surface exactly how it has come out and then fold it in half, taking the leading edge of the polymer and folding it onto the back edge. Use the same orientation each time and be sure to position the folded edge against the rollers. The blend should be perfect each time.

4. Jeff Dever has some great advice about how to keep the Skinner Blend in a rectangle as the edges thin out. He squishes each end in, making it thicker, so that it stays in line with the middle.

5. Using the same orientation, roll the folded sheet through your pasta machine, and then refold and repeat until the blend is evenly gradated and all streaks have disappeared. This could take twenty to twenty-five passes.

Partially Mixed Skinner Blend by Sandra McCaw

1. Condition several colors of polymer (six are shown below) and cut them into triangles of various widths but the same height. Assemble the triangles in an alternating pattern so that they form a rectangle.

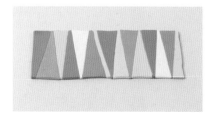

2. Roll the sheet through the pasta machine; then fold in half, keeping the same orientation.

3. Roll the resultant sheet through the pasta machine. Continue folding and rolling for about five or six times. This will create a sheet where the colors meet but do not blend completely from one to the other; when cut, the sheet's edge has a "thready" appearance. (See step 1 of The Floating Leaves Earrings on page 34.)

Multicolor Skinner Blend by Dayle Doroshow

1. Sheet several colors of polymer and cut triangles from each as described previously. Reassemble the triangles, as shown, and trim to make a rectangle. Gently press the seams to help them adhere together.

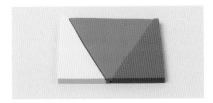

2. With your pasta machine at the thickest setting, align the rectangular sheet to the rollers so that all colors are touching them. Roll the sheet through once, to make sure the triangles don't separate, and then fold the resultant sheet in half, making sure that the two edges, perpendicular to the fold, of the same color meet.

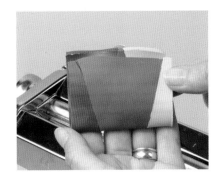

3. Using the same orientation, roll the folded sheet through your pasta machine, and then refold and repeat until the blend is evenly gradated and all streaks have disappeared. This could take twenty to twenty-five passes through the pasta machine.

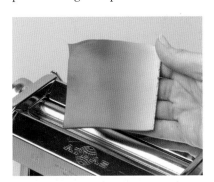

Controlling the Skinner Blend by Sarah Shriver

1. To achieve a more elongated transition between the colors, curve the edges slightly as you cut pieces; then lay them alongside each other and join the seams as shown in the top left assembly shown below right. Add in other colors to shift the hues and the blend. The top right assembly incorporates a subtle tan to mute the brightness of the white, and a buttery yellow to shift part of the blend toward the green spectrum. The bottom left assembly shifts further into the greener colors by increasing the amount of yellow polymer and adding a corner of darker green, but it becomes overall lighter by increasing the amount of unsaturated colors. The bottom right assembly just shows that neatness doesn't count! The blending of colors is based on the layout of the polymer, not on how neat and tidy the edges or seams are. Once you understand the theory of how it works, you don't even need to use a blade or make a perfect square or rectangle.

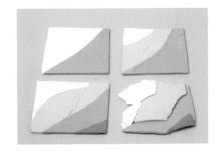

2. The migrating colors and values derived from blending one color into another, using this technique, provide a fantastic way to help understand the properties of colors.

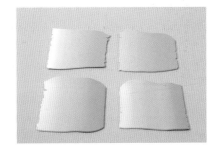

ATTRACT YOUR OPPOSITE
Leslie Blackford and Sandra McCaw

When Sandra McCaw called and asked to work with Leslie Blackford, it seemed an unlikely pairing. Sandra, with her strong background in graphic design, likes to follow a schedule, set goals for herself, and work tightly—not only in the pristine manner of her jewelry, but also in her workspace. Leslie, on the other hand, works intuitively and spontaneously in a sea of scrap polymer and smashed canes. Yet despite these differences, in fact because of their differences, each held a kind of fascination for the other.

Any schoolkid can tell you that, when dealing with magnetism, opposites attract. But what happens when two completely opposite approaches to polymer collide? As Sandra and Leslie discovered, tackling a creative project from a new point of view can open up new possibilities—for the project at hand and for future work. In the end, they created a work of art that represents the best of both of their worlds.

OPPOSITE/COLLABORATIVE PROJECT: Leslie Blackford and Sandra McCaw, *The Carousel of Animalia Delights*, 2011; polymer, metal-threaded rod and tube, and wire; 13 x 4 x 4 inches (33 x 10 x 10cm). Photograph by Richard K. Honaman Jr.

SHOWCASE LESLIE BLACKFORD

I have loved making things with polymer ever since I was a little girl. I am lucky to be part of a creative family who always encouraged me to do my own thing. I prefer to work in polymer because of its instant gratification and amazing versatility. Polymer allows me to go in so many directions—in fact, so many that sometimes it's hard to choose just one. I love knowing that the chunk of polymer in front of me can be anything I want it to be.

I feel most comfortable exploring creative ideas and expressing myself through sculpture. If I have spent the day walking around our property, for example, my hands might sculpt a whimsical turtle perched on the back of an opossum. The troops of carnival creatures I create emerged when I saw the effects of bullying on students who seemed different. I think people connect with the work that I do because I am willing to allow personal emotions and experiences to flow through my hands and become visible in polymer.

LEFT: *Wisdom and the Whip-Poor-Will*, 2010, split oak, moss, and polymer, 12 x 8 x 8 inches (30.5 x 20.5 x 20.5cm). Photograph by Todd Hodges. I collaborated with my father, master basket maker Randy Seymour, to create this sculpture. By example, he taught me to respect all things that live on this earth with us. Our outdoor times when I was a child were travels in wonderland.

ABOVE: *Pods*, 2011; polymer and ephemera, dimensions variable. Photograph by Todd Hodges. I've always wanted to create a series of pods that draw from nature—but don't exactly replicate nature—and include hidden surprises.

Damn Everything but the Circus, 2009; polymer and wood; 7½ x 5½ x 6 inches (19 x 14 x 15cm).
Photograph by Todd Hodges. I wanted this piece to convey that maybe the grass isn't always greener on the other side. This pig and cat have run away to join the circus, but after living the lives of carnies, they realize that it is not as carefree as they had imagined.

SHOWCASE SANDRA MCCAW

With my background in graphic design, precise geometric caning with polymer was a natural fit for me. It was thrilling to translate my experience in the graphic arts to a three-dimensional medium that I could hold in my hands, mixing colors instinctively rather than choosing from swatches produced by printing companies. During my search for a way to express my love of color and pattern with polymer—and how the two affected one another—I was drawn to the strip panels of gradated colors in the quilts of Michael James. I wondered how sheets of gradated polymer, stacked and cut into geometric shapes, would translate into a final design. The results surprised and delighted me. I had found my vehicle.

LEFT: Earrings from the *Floating Leaves* series, 2010; polymer, 23K gold leaf, and gold-filled wire; 2½ x ¾ inches (6.5 x 2cm). Photograph by Hap Sakwa. The "Floating Leaves" series has been an adventure for me, allowing me to escape from my symmetrical tendencies.

ABOVE: *Untitled*, 2010; polymer, 23K gold leaf, and gold-filled wire; 3½ x ½ inches (9 x 1.3cm). Photograph by Hap Sakwa. The bold, graphic elements of this piece are a throwback to my early days as a graphic designer.

Autumn, from the *Floating Leaves* series, 2011; polymer, 23K gold leaf, gold-filled wire, redwood, and glass beads; 5 x 18 inches (12.5 x 45.5cm). Photograph by Hap Sakwa. I'm pleased with the progression of movement and flow with each new piece in this series.

"When I get an idea for something that I want to make I don't
do much planning. I just jump in with both feet."

The Good, the Bad, and the Ugly Sculpture

When I get an idea for something that I want to make, I don't do much planning. I just jump in with both feet. I pull from my emotions, the ideas in my head, and the inspiration around me. Often my sculptures reflect my mood—even when that wasn't my original intention. With this in mind, I felt it would be fun to make a sculpture that allowed me to put out a "sign" expressing how I was feeling on any given day. And given the rules of society, which teach us to look and act a certain way, having this tool allows me to conform when I need to, but still express how I feel.

SUPPLIES

- polymer toolbox (see page 16)
- **polymer:** 4 oz. (113.5g) beige; 4 oz. (113.5g) scrap; 2 oz. (57g) translucent; 1 oz. (28g) ultra blue; 1 oz. (28g) red; ½ oz. (14g) brown; ½ oz. (14g) white; pinch of green and yellow (I used Kato Polyclay, as its superior strength makes the wearable art I create more durable.)
- knitting needle, US #5 (3.75mm), or blunt-tip tool
- globe lightbulb, G 16.5
- needle tool
- black glass beads, 10mm (5)
- piece of linen or coarse muslin cloth
- liquid polymer
- old toothbrush

Optional
- raw umber oil paint
- paper towel or soft cloth

OPPOSITE: Leslie Blackford, *The Good, the Bad, and the Ugly*, 2011; polymer and glass bulb; 4½ x 3 x 2½ inches (11.5 x 7.5 x 6.5cm). Photograph by Richard K. Honaman Jr.

THE HEADS

1. Roll a 2 oz. (57g) piece of conditioned beige polymer into the shape of a small egg. Using a knitting needle, start a hole in the bottom of the head. Gradually widen this hole by making circular strokes inside the bottom of the head. The hole should be large enough to accommodate the threaded end of the bulb. Place the head onto the end of the bulb then squeeze, using gentle but firm pressure, making sure the threaded part of the bulb leaves an exact impression inside the head.

   TIP: Form a ring out of scrap polymer and place the bulb firmly onto the polymer so the bulb stands straight up without wobbling. The base will hold the bulb and head in place, allowing you to work on the head hands-free.

2. Pinch an even amount of polymer from opposite sides of the head to create the ears. Define the area of the ear by making a shallow mark with the needle tool at both the top and bottom of each ear. Further define the inside of the ears by using a blunt tool like a knitting needle.

3. Use the needle tool to mark where the nostrils and eyes will be placed. Gently pinch the polymer between the marks made for the eyes, pulling a small amount of it forward to make the ridge of the nose. Slightly flatten the bottom of the ridge to create a triangular shape for the tip of the nose. Use the needle tool to make small holes for the nostrils.

4. Insert the needle tool into the marks made for the eyes. Widen the hole by moving the tool in a circular motion. Repeat on both sides of the face. Place a glass bead onto the end of the needle tool. Insert the bead sideways into an eye socket. This will secure the bead and keep the holes hidden from view.

   Roll a marble-size piece of beige polymer into a small ball, and then flatten it. Slice it in half to make eyelids. Place an eyelid so it covers about one-quarter of the eye (glass bead). Smooth out the polymer on the outside of the lid. Repeat for the other eye.

   NOTE: The placement of the lids is very important to the expression of the face. The direction that you point the lids will make the face look happy, sad, excited, and so on. See Capturing Emotions, opposite, for inspiration.

5. Form two small strips of beige polymer for eyebrows; they add character and a little more whimsy to the face. Use a needle tool to add a hairlike appearance to the eyebrows.

Make two indentations on the face to represent the length of the mouth. Use the needle tool to make a shallow line from one point to the other. Apply lines on the corners of the mouth in an upward direction. Cure the head on the bulb according to manufacturer's instructions. Allow the head to cool, and then unscrew from the bulb.

6. Repeat steps 1–5 to create the other two heads, drawing inspiration from the Capturing Emotions chart or your own imagination. I used 2 oz. (57g) beige polymer with a pinch of red to create the Bad Head, and 2 oz. (57g) translucent polymer with pinches of green and yellow to create the Ugly Head.

CAPTURING EMOTIONS

You can completely change the expression of a face by slightly manipulating the direction of the eyelids and the mouth. A small variation in the placement of these features can make a very dramatic change in the entire mood of a figure.

Playful
Fully cover one eye with an eyelid and place the second eyelid over one-quarter of the other eye. Add a shallow curved line for the mouth.

Surprised
Place the lids on the upper part of the eye; then raise them in the center, creating a wide-open eye. Open the mouth with a needle tool.

Angry
Slant the eyelids from the nose upward. Slant the eyebrows closer to the nose. Form an upside-down U shape for the mouth.

Indifferent
Place the lids evenly across the eye. Form a straight line for the mouth.

Sad
Slant the lids down on the outside of the eye. Place the eyebrows farther apart and follow the direction of the lid. Form a straight line for the mouth; then bring one end downward.

Sleepy
Place the lids so they cover about three-quarters of the eyes, slanting them only slightly. Form a small opening for the mouth.

THE BODY

1. Cover the bulb with 1 oz. (28g) of thoroughly conditioned scrap polymer, rolled to a thin setting. Squeeze the polymer around the bulb to make sure no air is trapped between the polymer and the bulb.

    Carefully cut away the excess polymer, and then smooth the surface. Flatten the polymer on the rounded end of the bulb; it should be able to stand on its own. Pierce a hole in the bottom of the polymer to allow any trapped air to escape during curing.

2. Roll out a sheet of ultra blue polymer on the thickest setting on your pasta machine. Repeat with red polymer to create a second sheet. Trim the ends so they are straight. Stack the sheets neatly on top of each other. Using an acrylic brayer, roll across the surface of the top layer to eliminate any air pockets that may be trapped between the layers. Cut this stack in half; then cut each half in half. Stack the cut sections on top of one another, making sure the colors alternate, creating a striped cane eight layers tall.

3. Cut several slices from the stack, placing them side by side onto the remaining scrap polymer sheet cut away in step 1. Lengthen and thin the sheet by rolling it through the pasta machine, lining the stripes up perpendicular to the rollers, starting with the thickest and working down to thinner settings. If you'd like to texture the polymer and give it a more realistic cloth look, place a piece of muslin or linen onto the striped sheet for the final roll through the pasta machine on a medium setting. Remove the cloth.

4. Cut several pieces of the striped "fabric" and, laying them as evenly as possible, cover the entire bulb. Tuck the excess polymer neatly under the bottom of the bulb. Trim away all polymer from the threaded end of the bulb.

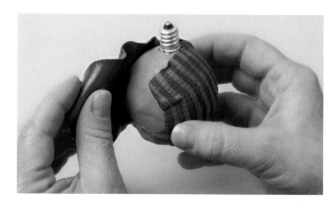

5. Roll out a small log of the beige polymer, about ½ inch (13mm) in diameter by 3 inches (7.5cm) long. Cut a rectangle of the striped fabric that will wrap the cylinder, leaving a bit of beige polymer exposed on each end for the hands. Measure and cut the log in half; then cut one end of each half on the diagonal. This will create the shoulder and allow the arm to lie flush with the rest of the body.

Add detail to suggest the hands by slightly flattening the exposed area of beige polymer at the end of each arm. Use the needle tool to make indents and lines in the polymer where the fingers would be.

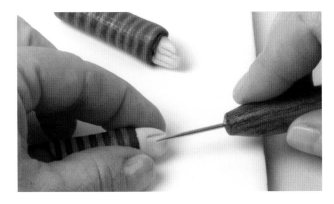

6. Apply a very small dot of liquid polymer to the end of each arm. Use firm pressure to attach the arms to the body. Position the arms close to the body so they are less susceptible to breakage. Retexture any part of the body with the muslin or linen cloth.

7. To create a base for your figure, thoroughly mix ½ oz. (14g) brown and ½ oz. (14g) white; roll it into a ball and then flatten it. Texture the surface with an old toothbrush, which creates a nice matte finish. Apply a small amount of liquid polymer to the center of the base. Center the body onto the base and apply slight pressure to make sure there is a strong connection between the two surfaces. Make the signs (as shown on page 26) with scrap polymer impressed with small rubber letter stamps. Create the bases for the heads from scrap polymer molded to accommodate the openings in the bottoms of the heads. Cure all pieces according to the manufacturer's instructions.

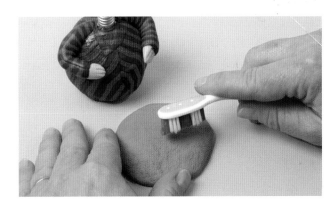

OPTIONAL

Antiquing is a simple technique that yields a dramatic effect and makes the piece look old and worn. I like to use raw umber oil paint, as it lends a rich, translucent effect. Use an old toothbrush to paint the surface of the piece. Apply paint generously, making sure to push it into every crack and crevice. Use a paper towel or soft cloth to wipe away all the excess paint. Let the paint cure for 24 hours.

Floating Leaves Earrings

When designing a line of jewelry, I usually begin with several sketches. Sometimes they're new drawings, but I often look back through journals where I've sketched objects that have interested me over the years and work from those. Next to experimenting with color and pattern, working out the fabrication of ideas is what I love best. I enjoy the challenge of getting from paper to polymer. Throughout this process I ask myself many questions: What other materials might I incorporate? How do I make it durable? I think about size, scale, and balance. I'm a planner, and I often ask—and answer—most of my questions before I touch the polymer.

I strive to translate, into concrete form, the colors and patterns I've absorbed throughout my life. I want the colors I've chosen for a piece—inspired, for example, by an early morning walk through gently falling snow in the depths of a hemlock grove—to evoke in the viewer the same feeling of calm I felt during that walk. Every aspect of our lives, every emotion, every choice and experience influences our process of creating art. When I'm successful, the essence of these moments is revealed.

SUPPLIES

- polymer toolbox (see page 16)
- **polymer:** 3 oz. (85g) teal; 2 oz. (57g) white; 2 oz. (57g) green; 2 oz. (57g) russet (I used Fimo Classic, as I find it maintains a crisp, clean pattern within a cane.)
- 23K gold leaf or gold-colored metallic leaf sheet

- graph paper
- half-hard, gold-filled round wire, 20-gauge
- wire cutters
- chain-nose pliers
- liquid polymer
- fine-pointed paintbrush
- polyurethane

- fine-tipped permanent marker
- metal knitting needle, US #10 (6mm)
- metal file (fingernail file works great)

Optional
- textured swatch of fabric, 4 x 8 inches (10 x 20.5cm)

OPPOSITE: Sandra McCaw, *Floating Leaves*, 2011; polymer, 23K gold leaf, and gold-filled wire; 3 x 1¼ inches (7.5 x 3cm). Photograph by Richard K. Honaman Jr.

THE EARRINGS

1. Set aside 1 oz. (28g) of teal polymer. Mix one-third of the white with one-third of each of the three colors to give you a tinted version of each color. Create a Partially Mixed Skinner Blend sheet by following the instructions on page 18. Cut 4 equal sections across the colors of the blended sheet; then stack the slices, staggering the colors. The staggering of the blended sheets will create a cane that resembles the ikat patterns often seen in fabric.

2. Roll 1 oz. (28g) of teal polymer through the pasta machine at the thickest setting. Cut 4⅛-inch (3mm) lengthwise slices from the ikat cane; place them side-by-side onto the teal sheet, mirroring the pattern. Roll this assembly through your pasta machine a few times, changing direction each time and reducing the thickness until the sheet is about ³⁄₃₂-inch (2mm) thick, thereby stretching the pattern. You may want to add a second backing sheet to stretch the pattern further. In the last pass, the stripes should be oriented perpendicular to the pasta machine rollers, and the resulting sheet should be at least 2 x 4 inches (5 x 10cm).

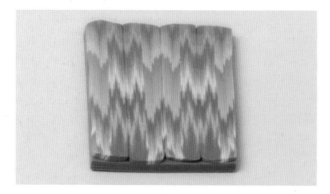

Repeat this process three or four times, giving you a selection of patterned sheets to work with.

TIP: I like to roll my sheets with a piece of textured fabric on the final pass to give the leaves an interesting surface.

3. Orient one of your ikat-patterned sheets so the pattern is on the diagonal. Curve a flexible blade and cut the outside edge of a leaf, keeping the blade steady while cutting through the polymer. Cut the polymer again to create the inside of the half-leaf shape.

4. Using one of the three colors for your leaf, roll a cylinder approximately ⅛ inch (3mm) in diameter by 1½ inches (3.8cm) long. Set the sheet of gold leaf on your work surface; then place the polymer cylinder onto one edge of the leaf and roll until covered. Press the gold leaf to the cylinder so that it is adhered. Roll the gold-leaf-covered cylinder into a thin, tapered "vein," pointing the end.

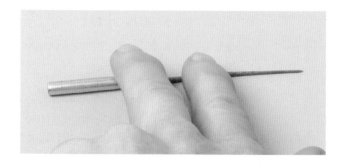

5. Place the vein along the inside edge of the half-leaf shape with the thinner, pointed end at the bottom of the leaf. Leaving about ⅛ inch (3mm) extending beyond the top of the leaf, cut off any excess vein.

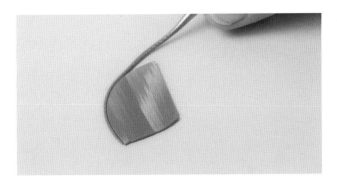

6. Lay the first half leaf on top of a second ikat sheet, orienting the ikat patterns in opposite directions. Using the inside edge of the half leaf as a template, cut the second half of the leaf.

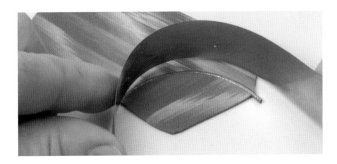

Position the two halves together with the vein in the middle. Press the parts together so they are connected. Trim the outside edges to form leaf shapes. Make several more leaves of varying sizes. Be sure to orient half of the leaves to the right and half to the left.

7. Choose 2 leaves that would make a good pair of earrings, one facing right and the other facing left. On a piece of graph paper, line up the top point of 1 leaf on a horizontal line and at an intersecting vertical line. Make marks at these points. Repeat for the second earring, leaving space between the two.

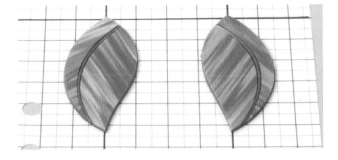

8. Determine how long you want the finished earrings to be, allowing length for the curve of the earring, the back of the earwire (the part that hangs behind the ear), 1 inch (2.5cm) for sandwiching between the leaf and the backing, and a little extra for good measure. Cut 2 lengths of 20-gauge gold-filled wire at the determined measurement.

Using chain-nose pliers, bend the end of one length of wire at a 90-degree angle; this bend will help hold the wire securely in the polymer. Working from 1-inch (2.5cm) above the 90-degree bend, begin to curve the wire so it follows the vein and exits the top of the leaf at the same point the vein does, as if it is an extension of the vein.

Repeat for the second leaf, making sure both wires intersect the vertical lines for each leaf on the same horizontal plane so they match.

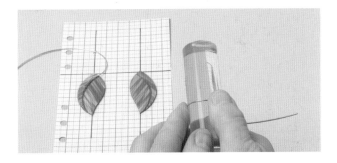

TIP: Use a template, such as a thick acrylic rod, to create equal curves in the wire.

9. Roll the remaining teal polymer to a medium thickness; this will be the backing of your earrings. Place the sheet along a horizontal line on your graph paper.

NOTE: A medium thickness will support an embedded 20-gauge wire; if you change the wire, you can change the thickness of the polymer.

Using the back of the flexible blade, and following the lines drawn on the graph paper, carefully make three guidelines in the polymer for each leaf: one horizontally ¼ inch (6mm) down from the top edge, and two vertically.

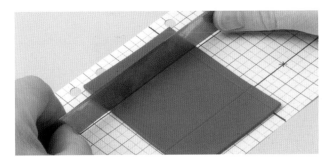

10. Hold a leaf above the backing. Position it so the top point is at the intersection of the horizontal and vertical line and the bottom point lines up with the vertical line. Place the corresponding wire under the leaf, making sure the wire is intersecting the same vertical and horizontal lines on the graph paper as it was earlier.

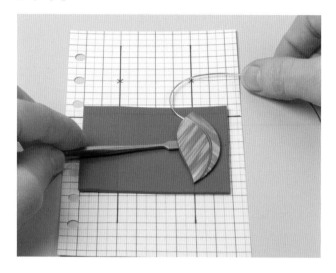

Apply a dab of liquid polymer to the wire and press the wire into the polymer so it is flush with the backing layer. Place the leaf into position on top of the wire and press gently to secure all of the layers together. Repeat for the second leaf.

11. Using your flexible blade, carefully cut away the excess backing polymer. Carefully transfer the earrings to your baking surface. Cure the earrings according to manufacturer's instructions. Once they are cured and cooled, use a fine-pointed paintbrush to coat the gold-leaf vein with polyurethane; this will prevent the gold leaf from tarnishing.

12. Line up the earrings on the graph paper once again. Using a fine-tipped permanent marker, place a mark on the wire at the point where it intersects the vertical lines. Place this mark at the top of the curve of a knitting needle; then bend the wire to form an earwire.

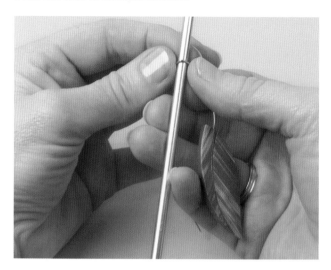

Adjust the back of the earwire in a pleasing curve. Adjust to hang correctly. Trim the wire if necessary and file the end. Repeat for the second earring.

Sandra took the ikat caning concept and the leaf shape in a more complex direction to create this beautiful and expressive necklace (below) and brooch (left). Photographs by Hap Sakwa

The Carousel of Animalia Delights

Sandra and Leslie did very little planning before arriving at the Outer Banks. Leslie had sent an image of a work of art that inspired her during a trip to Madrid (*The Garden of Earthly Delights* by Hieronymus Bosch). Sandra thought it was a pretty wild piece yet understood Leslie's attraction because she was very familiar with Leslie's work. She agreed to use this as a starting point.

The trust and respect they have for each other allowed the partners to venture into areas unknown and allowed the collaboration to flow—in spite of Sandra's fear that she would slow Leslie down, and despite Leslie's concern that she tends to be impatient and sometimes rushes the process. As the week progressed and their design evolved, they had moments when they disagreed, yet each knew when to relinquish control and let the other one lead.

Negotiating the Workspace

Leslie arrived at the house ahead of Sandra, and rather than selecting a place to work, she waited for Sandra to arrive the next day. Once together, they assessed the remaining workspace options and proceeded to take over a small balcony that overlooked the great room and main dining area of the house. Leslie was accustomed to working in and among people but understood Sandra's need for a quieter environment; Sandra stressed the importance of seclusion yet understood the need to still be part of the group. Through their compromise, they were able to overhear all conversations, observe most groups and the activities going on during the day and evening, and swoop down to be part of all things they wanted to be part of, yet they were not interrupted at critical stages of development.

The two set up their table, divided it in half, and started working out a plan. The images and ideas flowed freely, and the design evolved minute by minute.

Sandra lines everything up and keeps a clean space to work in; Leslie spreads out and piles things on top of things, yet she always knows where every tool and color of polymer can be found.

Opening to New Possibilities

Sandra and Leslie began the collaborative project by
evaluating their inspirational image, the beginnings of a
palette, some canes Sandra had brought with her, and some
sketches they had quickly rendered. They determined that a
support for the base would be needed, but they wanted it to
"feel" light. Leslie's prior work included creating translucent
caricatures over a glass lightbulb or votive candleholder, so
they decided this would be a good place to start.

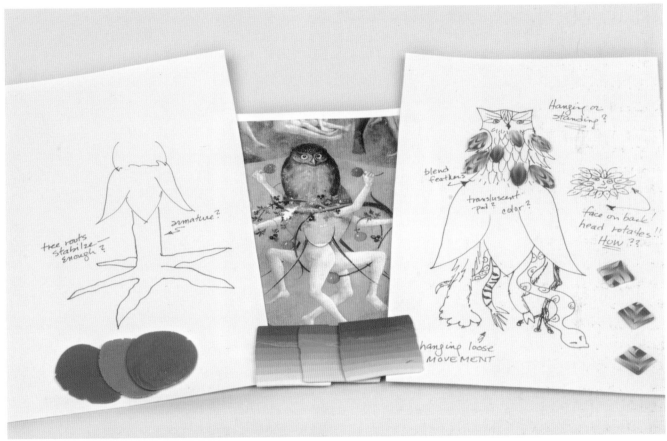

TOP: Leslie covered the votive candleholder with translucent polymer and cured it; then she carefully
removed the votive holder by slicing the polymer. She didn't worry about the slit in the polymer, as she
knew it would be covered.

ABOVE: Focusing on Leslie's inspirational image (Hieronymus Bosch's *The Garden of Earthly Delights*)
helped Sandra select a palette for the canes she brought with her to North Carolina.

*"Engaging in—not just observing—Leslie's spontaneous, playful approach has influenced
how I approach my own work. Also, I was able to literally expand my reach by working
on a relatively large piece with moving parts. It's good to change your point of view
every now and again."*

—*Sandra*

Combining Talents, Dividing the Work

While mixing colors to cover the translucent pod, the pair decided the translucent peach needed to be a bit darker. Sandra added some stiff orange Fimo to the mix of soft peach Kato and, with her mind focused on fully blending the new color, rolled it quickly through the pasta machine. Leslie stopped her midway through the blending process, already envisioning images of the legs that would be created later in the week, and remarked, "It looks just like a tiger's fur coat!"

Just like that she had the perfect piece of polymer to use for one of the sculpture's many legs. Having another person engaged in a project can open your mind to other possibilities as you work and keep you from focusing too intently on a specific step.

Sandra wanted to replicate the feel of *The Garden of Earthly Delights* for the decorative layer of the outside of the base. She combined a bit more opaque polymer to half of the translucent orange, making it a shade darker, and then added a pinch of glitter to both polymers to add sparkle. The two colors were used to create a translucent striped cane. Sandra pinched both ends to form a petal shape and carefully cut 8 slices.

Sandra draped 8 petals over the translucent base and ruffled the edges with her fingers, as you would press the edges of a piecrust. The piece at this stage was cured in a bed of cornstarch—to support the roundness and to assure that the petals would remain ruffled.

Leslie created a tree to hold the pod and used a metal tube for support and to keep the tree trunk completely straight. She covered the tube with scrap polymer to form the tree shape and then added a layer of realistic bark made from polymer. (See Technique: Fashioning Tree Bark on page 41 for information on making this realistic element.)

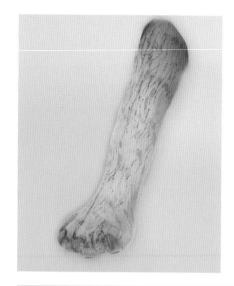

RIGHT TOP: By stopping Sandra mid blend, Leslie was able to capture the essence of a tiger's leg. Texturing with a needle tool transformed the polymer into fur. **RIGHT MIDDLE:** While the cane was quite large (3 x 2 inches [7.5 x 5cm]), Sandra ran the slices through the pasta machine to lengthen and thin petals and then carefully stretched them to the perfect size to cover the base. **RIGHT BOTTOM:** Sandra used a rubber-tipped sculpting tool that Leslie had brought to adjust how the petals would lie on the base.

TECHNIQUE: FASHIONING TREE BARK

1. Prepare polymer in a variety of thicknesses. Notice Leslie's unusual choice of adding a darker blue to gold and brown sheets of polymer. This combination may be surprising, but upon closer observation you, too, can see unexpected colors in nature.

2. Stack the sheets of polymer to form a striped cane. (Instructions for a similarly striped cane can be found in step 2 in The Body on page 30.)

3. Prepare a sheet of coordinating polymer. Cut ¼-inch- (6mm-) thick slices of the striped cane and place them side by side on the sheet. Drag an old comb through the resulting sheet, following the line of the stripes.

4. With your finger, dab white paint into the lines created with the comb; then, using a flexible blade, shave off thin pieces of the "bark" and place them onto a sheet of scrap polymer.

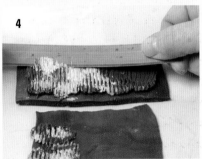

Sandra watched in amazement as Leslie, in a matter of moments, created bark that was almost indistinguishable from the real thing.

Refining the Vision

The team decided the tree needed a rock to stabilize the piece and support the roots. Leslie created the rock from translucent polymer mixed with embossing powder. (For instructions on forming realistic rocks, see steps 1–4 in The Rocks on page 54.) The tree was cured according to the manufacturer's instructions, making sure that it stayed completely level, using batting for support.

Leslie and Sandra knew they wanted an owl to be perched on top of the pod, so Leslie quickly created one from solid polymer in a size that she felt closely matched their sketches. However, once it was finished, they determined that it would make the piece too top heavy, so (taking a cue from Dayle and Sarah's collaborative project, shown on page 68) Leslie resculpted the owl in Sculpey UltraLight. This owl turned out to be too small. After some discussion, Sandra remarked that the owl should be only 25–30 percent smaller than the pod. Leslie crafted a third and final owl and added eyes. Robert

added just the right touch—a metal crown to top off the bird.

Sandra then spent two days applying a feather-type cane she had brought with her for inspiration, following the natural order of feathers on a fowl. Sandra used the smaller owl as a model so she could try out different ways of applying the feathers and test the size and shape of the feathers. The model also allowed Leslie to test whether oil paint—a staple of her sculptures—would work for this project before they committed to the larger owl. While Leslie wasn't used to working in such a meticulous manner, she did find that using the model allowed her to appreciate how Sandra perceived scale. In the end, however, they decided that oil paint was not right for this project—it was too dark, and some of the colors in the feathers were lost.

Once all testing was complete, Sandra applied the feathers to the owl in stages, curing it multiple times to retain the pristine nature of the cane slices.

ABOVE LEFT: Leslie sculpted mushrooms and placed them here and there at the tree base after she and Sandra decided it needed more earthly additions. The tree was then cured again. **ABOVE MIDDLE:** Leslie embedded glass taxidermy eyes for a realistic look. **ABOVE RIGHT:** A spatula-shaped dental tool allowed Sandra to apply the feathers without leaving a single fingerprint—a testament to her style of working.

"Even though Sandra and I work in completely different ways, I felt like we had the same vision of what the finished piece would look like. Sandra was painstakingly applying feathers to the owl while I was forming legs, and I had an epiphany. . . . I should pay closer attention when developing detailed aspects of my sculptures, like fur."

—Leslie

Finding an Unexpected Solution

Sandra and Leslie consulted frequently with Robert over the mechanics of having the owl's head turn. On the third day they had a breakthrough—the head would remain attached to the owl and the pod would spin. This change would also allow the legs planned for the pod to move in a much more whimsical way. This was an unexpected, yet thrilling, solution—not to mention a much easier way to work out the mechanics.

They chose a threaded metal rod that could fit into the metal tube in the tree. The pod was drilled through to accommodate the rod. The owl was drilled from the bottom toward the top for about 2 inches (5cm), but they were careful not to go all the way through. The tube was cut to 1 inch (2.5cm) above the tree for scale.

While Sandra was meticulously placing feathers on the owl, Leslie quickly sculpted dozens of animal legs to hang from underneath the pod. She decided to fashion the legs in simple shapes, created from logs of scrap polymer covered with solid polymer or very basic canes, such as stripes for a zebra, spots for a leopard, translucent pink for a pig, and so forth. (For instructions on making a whimsical leg, see Technique: Creating a "Snake Leg" on page 44.) She inserted a twisted wire with a loop into the top of each leg prior to curing so the leg could be attached to the pod and allowed to swing freely.

Sandra wanted to contribute to the sculptural part of the piece, so she created a very realistic frog leg. Wendy was enchanted with the piece and offered a tentacle to join the leg "party."

ABOVE RIGHT: Leslie sculpted so quickly she ended up with seven extra legs. These ended up being included in a collaborative wall piece created at a retreat held later that year. **RIGHT**: Robert's knowledge of cold connections proved invaluable as Sandra and Leslie worked through the mechanics of their piece.

TECHNIQUE: CREATING A "SNAKE LEG"

1. Create a Skinner Blend jelly roll of green and yellow and wrap it with a thin sheet of black and white polymer. (For instructions on forming a Skinner Blend jelly roll, see steps 1, 2, and 4 in Folded Beads on page 60.)

2. Reduce the cane by rolling it to a diameter of ¼ inch (6mm); then cut it into 6 equal lengths and combine. Repeat this process until the pattern reminds you of a snake's skin.

3. Cut thin slices of the cane and place them onto a sheet of scrap polymer. Roll the polymer through the pasta machine to smooth and elongate the pattern slightly.

4. Roll a snake shape of scrap polymer and cover it with the prepared sheet.

5. Cut a length of wire, form it into a loop, and twist the ends together. Place the twisted end into one end of the polymer snake. Cure the leg.

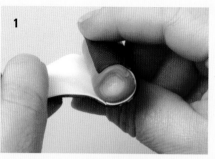

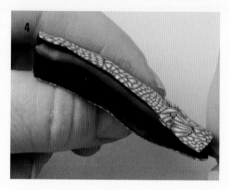

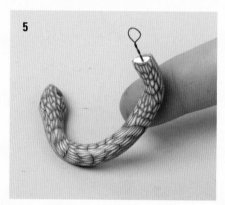

Completing the Collaboration

Leslie drilled tiny holes in the base of the pod and used a very thin wire to attach each of the legs. The wire was threaded through the loop on a leg, through the hole in the pod, and then twisted to secure.

Sandra carefully assembled the piece by placing the rod in the tube of the tree and adding a nut and washer to support the pod at the top of the tube. She lowered the pod onto the rod and added another nut to slightly lift the owl away from the pod. She applied two-part epoxy to the end of the rod to permanently affix the owl on top.

"When opposites attract there is a serious opportunity for growth. Leslie and Sandra joined forces at the intersection of spontaneity and process. They negotiated what, at times, was a circuitous route but, through communication and trust, created a complex and sophisticated hybrid of their very individual styles."

—Jeff

Leslie and Sandra spent a lot of time discussing the mechanics of the sculpture. Peals of delight were heard throughout the house when they finally figured out how fun it would be to have the legs move like a carousel.

RESPECT HIDDEN STRENGTHS
Cynthia Tinapple and Lindly Haunani

Cynthia Tinapple and Lindly Haunani have been friends for more than twenty years. They worked closely during the formative years of the National Polymer Clay Guild, frequently bouncing ideas back and forth during retreats and gatherings. Surprisingly, the two had never formally collaborated on a piece until now. Given the depth of their personal relationship, the challenge for this pair was distillation. Would each be able to recognize the particular strengths—both in herself and in her partner—that would make this collaboration a success?

Lindly always considers color and form first. When an idea strikes, she sets about making hundreds of components, sometimes backing herself into a corner, not knowing exactly how the pieces will fit together. Cynthia relies on her eye and a gut response to design, and admits that she can sometimes be "accommodating to a fault." Lindly's penchant for making many pieces and Cynthia's need to explore gave them many options, but in the end it was their respect for each other's strengths and the ability to be honest with one another that brought the piece together. Even down to the last day they were adding new and interesting elements—seemingly not wanting the journey to end.

OPPOSITE/COLLABORATIVE PROJECT: Cynthia Tinapple and Lindly Haunani, *A Walk Along the Beach*, 2010; polymer and embossing powder; 2 x 30 x 1 inches (5.1 x 76.2 x 2.5cm). Photograph by Richard K. Honaman Jr.

My impulse to create got rerouted into a communications career for practical reasons, but at home I have always been a maker and a visual artist. My dual-channel career continues to this day, even in my retirement—I work in the studio with polymer, and I communicate about it daily online through my blog, PolymerClayDaily.com. I claim both as my art forms.

Polymer has a physicality that immediately appealed to me when my daughter and I were making miniatures for her dollhouse in the late 1980s. Polymer is portable and easy to access. Mixing color in my hands is tactile and powerful, similar to the feeling I have when working on the computer.

While I enjoy wearing polymer jewelry, integrating polymer into objects in my home is what gives me the greatest pleasure. Two things make my decorating easier. First, my husband can do wonders with wood. Second, he grew up in a military family that moved frequently, and he refuses to move again. We don't worry about what prospective buyers might think about the embellishments we make to our home. Together we have made furniture, lamps, sinks, bowls, and wall decor that incorporate polymer. Living with our handiwork and sharing our art with visitors is our best reward.

LEFT: *It Is Well*, 2009; polymer and cherry; 10 x 8 x 8 inches (25.5 x 20.5 x 20.5cm). Photograph by Blair Davis and Cynthia Tinapple This cherry vase with transfers, created for the Synergy2 exhibit, celebrates the women in my family's history. Blair Davis turned the bowl. **ABOVE:** The polymer mosaic helped update the look of our front door and covered damaged wood. Realtors say that the entry sets the tone for a home, and visitors remark that "artists must live here" when they approach our door. Photograph by Blair Davis and Cynthia Tinapple

ABOVE: *Shisha*, 2011, polymer and walnut, 4 x 11 x 11 inches (10 x 28 x 28cm). Photograph by Blair Davis and Cynthia Tinapple. I created this Shisha bowl in anticipation of my trip to Nepal I to visit women working in polymer there. My head was spinning with Indian and Nepali embroidery designs. The bowl was turned by Blair Davis. **RIGHT:** Our casbah-style bathroom glows with a copper tub surround, polymer pendant lights, and an inlaid walnut bowl. Drawer pulls in the room match the inlay. Photograph by Blair Davis and Cynthia Tinapple

SHOWCASE LINDLY HAUNANI

My fascination, appreciation, and reverence for all things related to food was ignited in me when I was very young by my patient Hawaiian grandmother who lovingly gave me cooking lessons. Even now, I will hear Tutu's calm, wise voice telling me, "Wait until the bubbles on the edge pop before turning them over" or "The edge of a ripe mango will yield here when pressed gently." And now, more than fifty years later, I am still passionately inspired by food—both in the kitchen and in my studio.

I make my jewelry much in the same way I cook. I strive to respect and highlight the ingredients, while keeping things simple. Before putting a series of necklaces together I will amass hundreds of components in complementary shapes, colors, or variations (much in the same way a chef would prepare her *mise-en-place*) before embarking on the final stages of the pieces. Unlike a tray of carved vegetable crudités, the polymer pieces I fashion individually by hand have a tendency to last a lot longer.

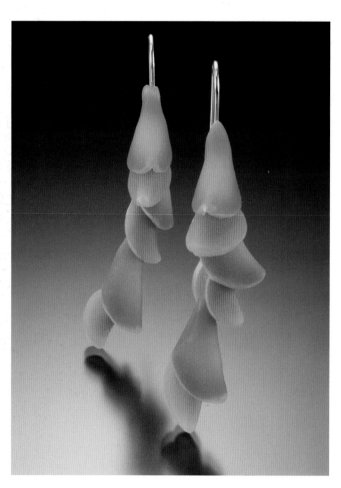

ABOVE: *Spring Bud Earrings*, 2009; polymer and sterling silver wire; 3¼ x ¾ inches (8.5 x 2cm). Photograph by Hap Sakwa. I used lightly tinted translucent polymer to make three different round canes that could be overlapped to resemble budding petals. **RIGHT:** *Ripple Leaf Necklace*, 2009; polymer with base metal-covered clasp; 1½ x 24 x ¼ inches (3.8 x 61 x 0.6cm). Photograph by Hap Sakwa. The spectacular leaf necklaces that Pier Volkous made in the early 1990s inspired this piece. The wavy leaf vein insert was designed to reiterate the wavy edges of the leaves.

Purple Petal Rope Necklace, 2008; polymer and elastic cording; 1½ x 60 inches (3.8 x 152.5cm). Photograph by Hap Sakwa. This necklace may be worn three different ways: as a long rope; doubled up, as a medium-length necklace; or tripled up, as a clustered choker. The long, curved tube beads allow for visual rest and flow between the clusters of petals.

"Once you see how easy it is to drill a hole and fill it with polymer, no floor or door or unsuspecting table will be safe. They can all become part of your canvas."

Rock On! Bowl

Many people assume that the polymer inlays that I have done in wood bowls (or on cabinet trim, sinks, and stairways) are the result of a laborious process. While it helps to have a woodworker spouse cut and drill pieces to perfect specifications, shortcuts can provide simple ways to integrate polymer into your decor. Be forewarned, however: Once you see how easy it is to drill a hole and fill it with polymer, no floor or door or unsuspecting table will be safe. They can all become part of your canvas.

I recommend that you choose an old piece of furniture or a thrifted wooden item for your first inlay project. Since you're experimenting, you'll have more fun if you stay away from precious bowls or furnishings. I purchased this wooden salad bowl for very little at a big box store. One of the joys of making faux pebbles is that there's no waste. Simply roll leftover pieces of one color into the next color. You get greater variety in your rocks and use up all your scraps.

SUPPLIES

- polymer toolbox (see page 16)
- **polymer:** 6 oz. (170g) translucent (I used Premo! Sculpey because it is easy to condition and cures with a matte finish.)
- wooden bowl
- pencil
- nail or center punch

- hammer
- masking tape
- drill bit, ¼-inch (6mm)
- variable-speed drill
- embossing powders: Ranger's black soot and seafoam white (see other color suggestions in Making Rock Colors, page 56)

- circle cutter, ⅝-inch (16mm)
- cardstock
- wood glue

Optional
- rocks (for texture)
- needle tool
- removable painter's tape

OPPOSITE: Cynthia Tinapple, *Rock On! Bowl*, 2011; polymer and acacia; 3 x 5½ x 5½ inches (7.5 x 14 x 14cm). Photograph by Richard K. Honaman Jr.

THE BOWL

1. Take a look at your wooden item and figure out how it would be best enhanced with rocks. In a regular pattern? Scattered randomly? Close to each other? Should the rocks be big or small or varied in size? Flat or rounded?

   Using a pencil, sketch your design or pattern, right onto the bowl. Place a nail or center punch in the center of the pencil mark and strike with a hammer to create a starter hole. The starter hole will give the drill bit a place to grip the wood. Wrap a piece of tape around the drill bit about ⅛ to ¼ inch (3 to 6mm) from the end of the bit. The tape will be your guide for how deep to drill into the wood; a shallow hole is sufficient.

2. Brace the bowl against a sturdy object, center the drill bit on the starter hole and begin drilling. Take care not to go entirely through the wood with the drill bit. (Should this happen, simply adjust your design!) Repeat, drilling 1 hole for each rock.

THE ROCKS

1. Condition 1 oz. (28g) of translucent polymer and cut a 3-inch- (7.5cm-) square sheet. Pour ¼ tsp. (1.2mL) black soot embossing powder onto the polymer. Using a finger, spread the powder over the polymer. Fold and roll the polymer by hand or in the pasta machine until the powders are evenly distributed through the polymer.

   TIP: Vary the amount of powder used and you'll be able to create a range of grays that make quite convincing rocks. (See Making Rock Colors on page 56 for additional recipes.)

2. To create a wishing stone or a stone with a line running through it, mix a small amount of translucent polymer, some seafoam white embossing powder, and ground pepper. Blend using the same method as in step 1.

3. Roll out the colored translucent polymer from step 1 on the thickest setting of your pasta machine. Using the circle cutter, cut out 5 circles. More layers will equal larger rocks.

   Roll out a thin sheet of the wishing-stone blend from step 2, and then cut out a circle or two. Layer the circles into a stack, placing the wishing-stone layers somewhere in between the layers of colored-translucent circles.

4. Round the edges of the stack. Begin to form the stack into a barrel shape; then continue rolling it between the palms of your hands until you have a ball shape and you can no longer see the individual layers. Flatten the ball between your palms. An irregular shape is more believable than a perfectly smooth, symmetrical one.

If the vein layer becomes wavy, tease it back into more of a straight line by pinching and pushing the surrounding polymer. Look at beach pebbles (if available) to see how lines usually form.

If you want surface texture on your faux rock, press the polymer onto a real rock to pick up roughness. Often the vein line is pitted on real rocks; you can simulate this by poking the light vein layer with a needle tool.

5. Add a nub of polymer the size of the drill hole; the nub will be used to glue the rock into the bowl. You may want to temporarily position the unbaked polymer pebbles on your bowl to see how it's going to look and to make sure the nubs or tabs on the rocks fit easily into the holes. Repeat steps 1–5 to create as many rocks as you would like for your bowl.

Place the rocks on cardstock and cure according to the manufacturer's instructions. Allow them to cool to room temperature. Apply a bit of wood glue into a hole and insert a rock into it. You may want to temporarily tape it in place while the glue dries.

OPTIONAL

If you want it to appear as though the rocks are passing through the bowl, drill holes completely through the bowl; cut the "rocks" in half, and then follow step 5 to finish the rocks and add them to your bowl.

MAKING ROCK COLORS

I use a palette of Ranger embossing powders in the following colors: black soot, seafoam white, antique linen, weathered wood, and milled lavender. Martha Stewart Crafts crystal fine glitter will add a realistic sparkle effect. When mixing in several powders, blend the colors together on the polymer with your finger before proceeding.

You can also add many other finely crushed ingredients that simulate rock materials to translucent polymer, including sand, spices, eggshells, and coffee grounds. When I need a consistent, predictable outcome, I limit myself to embossing powders.

Translucent polymer colored with embossing powders darkens a shade or two when it's baked. The colors are muted and perfectly simulate nature's palette. You may want to bake a small amount of each shade of colored polymer as samples. I enjoy having sample rocks on my work surface for reference and to use for texturing. A jagged rock impressed into the polymer will give your polymer real rocklike texture. Combine any leftovers for additional color variations. As in nature, nothing goes to waste!

Part Soot
⅛ tsp. (0.6mL) black soot, plus a pinch of walnut stain to 1 oz. (28g) translucent polymer
wishing line: ¼ tsp. (1.2mL) seafoam white and a bit of black pepper to 1 oz. (28g) translucent polymer

Rust
¼ tsp. (1.2mL) rust, plus a pinch of black soot to 1 oz. (28g) translucent polymer

Seafoam
¼ tsp. (1.2mL) seafoam white to 1 oz. (28g) translucent polymer

Soot
⅓ tsp. (1.6mL) black soot to 1 oz. (28g) translucent polymer

Walnut Stain
¼ tsp. (1.2mL) walnut stain to 1 oz. (28g) translucent polymer

Weathered Wood
¼ tsp. (1.2mL) weathered wood to 1 oz. (28g) translucent polymer
wishing line: ⅛ tsp. (0.6mL) seafoam white to ¼ oz. (7g) translucent polymer

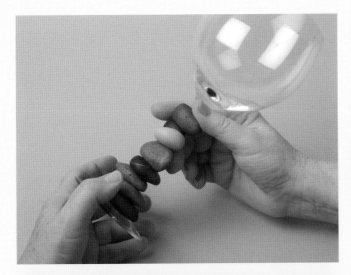

ABOVE LEFT: "Rocks" can be added to virtually anything, including the stems of these inexpensive wine glasses.

ABOVE RIGHT: Adding decorative handles to this wooden tray (above right) instantly turns it into a companion piece for the Rock On! Bowl. Photographs by Richard K. Honaman Jr.

*"Simple, graphic canes appeal to me as design components—
as the relationships between the individual beads and the stringing
rhythm take center stage in a design."*

Folded Bead Lei

My lifelong passions for color, cooking, and Hawaiian leis are recurring themes for me as an artist. One of my fondest memories from childhood is folding and pinching Chinese pot stickers. While working in my studio I often "sketch" by pinching and folding cane slices as a way to design new petal-like bead forms. What excites me most about the bead in this necklace is how it interlocks with the adjoining beads when strung and how the pearlized edges subtly reflect light.

Simple, graphic canes appeal to me as design components—as the relationships between the individual beads and the stringing rhythm take center stage in a design. After I designed the initial folded bead component and determined the scale of the beads, I experimented with five different food-inspired color combinations, literally making hundreds of components. I especially enjoy making the same design in different colors as a way of exploring the relationship between the chosen colors and the overall impact of the design. Three color combinations are listed on the pages that follow. Choose one or use them as inspiration to design your own.

OPPOSITE: Lindly Haunani, *Folded Bead Lei*, 2011; polymer and glass beads; 2 x 21 inches (5 x 53.5cm). Photograph by Richard K. Honaman Jr.

SUPPLIES

- polymer toolbox (see page 16)
- **polymer:** see Making Bead Colors on page 61 for amounts and colors (I used Premo! Sculpey because I like its range of primary colors and how well the colors blend together.)
- pin tool (I used a 1mm hat pin for its thin diameter and sharp point.)
- flexible beading wire, .018/.019 49-strand
- wire cutters
- crimp beads, 1 x 1mm (5)
- crimping pliers
- matte finish seed beads in a coordinating color, size 6/0 (45)
- crimp covers (4)

Optional
- chain-nose pliers

FOLDED BEADS

1. Create a Skinner Blend following the Two-Color Skinner Blend instructions on page 18 for each component of your chosen fruit/color combination. Cut the blend in half to create 2 sheets with equal blends.

Fold one of your blended sheets into thirds, matching the colors, and align the darkest end to your pasta machine. Roll the polymer through at the thickest setting. Change the setting on the pasta machine to medium, and roll the polymer through to elongate your blend. This will transform the Skinner Blend sheet into a long ribbon and add to the illusion of a subtle ombré pattern, or gradually shaded blend, in the finished cane.

2. Starting with the lightest end, trim to square off the short end of the ribbon. Using the polymer you trimmed off, fashion a ¹⁄₃₂-inch- (0.8mm-) diameter snake and align it to the squared-off end of the ribbon. This makes it easier to roll up the cane and decreases the possibility of air pockets occurring when the cane is reduced in size. Slowly roll the sheet up into a Skinner Blend jelly roll. Gently squeeze this cane to consolidate the polymer; then roll it on your work surface until the seam disappears.

3. Repeat step 1, folding the remaining half of your blended sheet and rolling it through the pasta machine to create a ribbon. Repeat step 2 to create a second Skinner Blend jelly roll, but this time start with the darkest end.

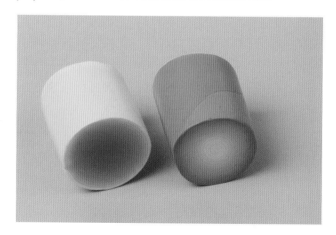

4. Create a sheet of polymer for the outline color, rolling it to the medium setting of your pasta machine; trim the front edge even. Place one Skinner Blend jelly roll on the front edge of this sheet of polymer; then gently roll this assembly forward, past where the seam of the outline color should be. Roll the polymer backward, which will create a line of demarcation where the sheet of polymer overlaps itself; trim the polymer at this mark. Join the two edges of the outline sheet in a butted seam and roll gently to smooth the polymer so no seam is evident.

Repeat to add an outline layer to the second Skinner Blend jelly roll cane.

5. Using an acrylic rod, exert firm pressure on the cylindrical cane to change it to a squared log. Flatten along the top of the log; then flip and repeat on the opposite side. Give the log a quarter turn, roll to flatten that side, and then flip it to the opposite side. Alternate rolling on each side until the cane is reduced to 1 x 1–inch (2.5 x 2.5cm) square. Repeat for the second cane.

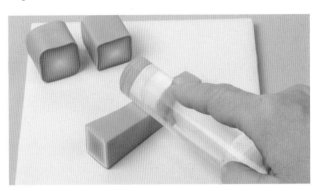

MAKING BEAD COLORS

When someone tells me that a piece of my jewelry looks edible, I consider that to be the ultimate compliment. Maybe that's why my color combinations are all inspired by food.

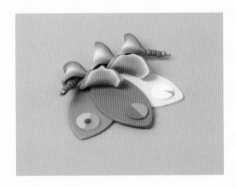

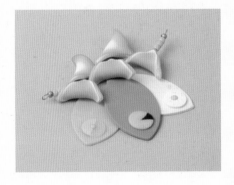

Watermelon

light color: 2 oz. (57g) white and ⅛ oz. (3.5g) candy pink

main color: 1 oz. (28g) cadmium red and 1 oz. (28g) candy pink

outline color: ½ oz. (14g) pearl, ½ oz. (14g) translucent, and ¹⁄₁₆ oz. (1.8g) green

Blueberry

light color: 2 oz. (57g) white and ⅛ oz. (3.5g) ultramarine blue

main color: 1 oz. (28g) ultramarine blue and 1 oz. (28g) fuchsia

outline color: ½ oz. (14g) pearl, ½ oz. (14g) translucent, and ¹⁄₁₆ oz. (1.8g) ultramarine blue

Star Fruit

light color: 2 oz. (57g) white and ⅛ oz. (3.5g) cadmium yellow

main color: 1¾ oz. (50g) cadmium yellow and ¼ oz. (7g) ultramarine blue

outline color: ½ oz. (14g) pearl, ½ oz. (14g) translucent, and ¹⁄₁₆ oz. (1.8g) cadmium yellow

6. Cut a ⅛-inch (3mm) slice from a square cane and coax the 2 opposing edges of the square together, and then flare the outer edges.

7. Insert a pin tool into the folded edge and continue coaxing and flaring the edges until it is anchored on the tip of the pin tool. The pin tool creates the stringing hole.

Repeat steps 6 and 7 to create more beads. To make a 22-inch- (56cm-) long necklace you will need about 50 beads—25 with the light centers and 25 with the dark centers. When slicing the cane, I like to reduce it further after a few slices are made, so the beads are formed in graduated sizes.

8. Cut a 2-inch (5cm) piece of the beading wire and thread on 1 crimp bead. Pass the end of the wire back through the crimp bead to form a loop. Place the crimp into the rear notch of the crimping pliers (the notch closest to the handles). Separate the wires inside the crimp. Close the pliers so the crimp bead is compressed and forms a crescent shape. Move the crescent into the notch in the front of the crimping pliers. Close the pliers to shape the crimp bead into a rounded bead shape. Trim any excess wire from the short end.

Cut a thicker (¼-inch [6mm]) slice from the cane to be used as the toggle bar for the necklace closure. Fold the cane slice in half diagonally and embed the wire loop into the polymer where the edges of the slice meet so that the

loop of the crimped wire faces out. Cure the beads and the toggle according to the manufacture's instructions and allow them to cool before stringing.

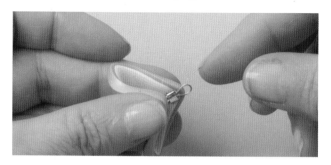

9. Cut a 30-inch (76cm) length of beading wire. Thread on a crimp bead, and then pass the end of the wire through the loop of beading wire embedded in the toggle bar made in step 8. Pass the end of the wire back through the crimp bead. Slide the crimp bead toward the toggle bar, keeping one end of the wire 1 inch (2.5cm) long. Crimp the crimp bead as you did in step 8.

Thread on about 1½ inches (3.8cm) of seed beads and then a crimp bead. Push the seed beads and crimp toward the first crimp bead so there is little space between them. Crimp the crimp bead. The crimp beads will offer more strength to the end of your necklace, and the extra seed beads will provide the length needed for passing the toggle bar through the toggle loop.

String on the petals in graduated order (if you chose to make smaller petals) as well as alternating dark- and light-center petals for interest in the finished piece. String enough petals to complete your finished length.

10. String on a few seed beads, 1 crimp bead, about 1 inch (2.5cm) of seed beads, 1 crimp bead, and then about 2 inches (5cm) of seed beads. Pass the beading wire back through the first crimp to form a loop of seed beads on the end. Test the loop to see if it will fit over the toggle bar. Adjust the amount of seed beads to either increase or decrease the size of the loop so the toggle bar can pass through the loop but not fall through easily once connected. Continue to pass the beading wire down the seed beads and through the second crimp bead. Tighten up the beads so there is little space between the bead and the loop, yet the necklace has a nice (not stiff) drape. Crimp the crimp beads to secure.

Using wire cutters, trim any excess beading wire from each end of the necklace. Using chain-nose pliers or the front notch of your crimping pliers, close crimp covers over the 4 crimped crimp beads for a nice finish.

FOLDING AND FORMING

I've pinched thousands of petal beads over the years and have learned these six important tips.

- The fresher the cane—less than a week old—the easier it will be to fold.
- Store the cane at its largest size; then reduce it to the size you plan to use (2- to 3-inch [5- to 7.5cm] segments) right before you plan to slice the cane.
- Cut slices slightly thicker than the final desired thickness; this allows for pinching.
- Before folding, gently squeeze and pinch the entire cane slice, starting at the middle and ending on the edges.
- Fold slowly, encouraging the polymer into the shape by alternating edges.
- Pay attention to the area where you are forming the hole and take time to make sure both edges of the polymer are adhered together for at least ⅛ inch (3mm). (This won't show when you string your necklace.)

Lindly's passion for food is brought to life in this alternative color combination—star fruit. The "recipe" for this colorway appears on page 61. Photograph by Richard K. Honaman Jr.

COLLABORATIVE PROJECT

A Walk Along the Beach

Cynthia and Lindly had limited discussions prior to the week at the beach and agreed only on a direction—jewelry—and finding a way to mesh their different working methods. Upon arrival at the house, they scouted out a place to work together. The table in the great room with the best ocean view was very appealing—the draw of the sea was strong. This prized location was already occupied by Dayle and Sarah, but with a bit of adjusting, room was made for all. In the end, the close proximity of two different collaborative teams worked to everyone's advantage.

Embracing an Open-Ended Approach

Cynthia and Lindly were inspired by the colors offered by Mother Nature (even in March during a nor'easter) and agreed they would work well for their palette. Neither was worried about formulating some kind of project from their work together. Lindly, a natural teacher, thought through what they were doing and quickly laid out the process as if she were creating steps for a workshop. Cynthia was used to presenting a critical snapshot every day on her blog, so she was confident she would visualize the project. A walk on the beach and a close look at how beach stones, shells, and debris piled up sparked ideas, but the two agreed the final design would evolve in its own time.

"As all chefs know—good ingredients in, great dish out. Cynthia and Lindly are makers. Their process was one of creating through playful, yet systematic, experimentation with a minimum of preplanning. Their history as friends provided the confidence to create, then edit and amend, their explorations, birthing new directions en route."

—Jeff

Acknowledging Differences in Process

Cynthia and Lindly decided that beach stones would provide the cornerstone of their project. However, when preparing their polymer ingredients for the stones, they realized that they have totally different approaches. Lindly started with measuring and building a systemized palette, as is her norm. By contrast, Cynthia looked at various rocks, determined what she liked, and then "reverse engineered," figuring out what she needed in order to arrive at a similarly pleasing mix or blend. Lindly's approach was proactive, while Cynthia's was more reactive. Cynthia allowed Lindly the time and space she needed to orient herself with the beach-stone palette.

Cynthia and Lindly shared a table with Dayle and Sarah. This not only gave both teams a chance for more input on their respective projects but also offered a delightful opportunity for Lindly and Sarah to try out new comedic material. Laughter was abundant.

Editing and Refining Color Concepts

After working independently for a while, the two compared palettes and agreed that Lindly's chosen colors were not usually found in rock material. It was difficult for Cynthia to watch Lindly struggle with stone colors, but then she realized she had not told Lindly that the embossing powders they were mixing changed the color significantly when cured. She suggested mixing small batches of translucent polymer with the different embossing powders and recording on the back of the cured samples the color and amount of embossing powder that was mixed in. After doing this, and discussing their colorways further, they edited their color selection, decided on a palette, and then experimented with form and shape, creating beach stones, cairnlike stacks of faux stones, lichens on a branch, and folded mosslike petals.

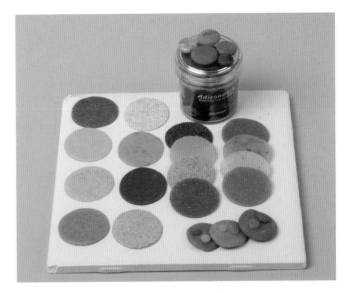

To the left is the palette in its raw state; the right shows the eight rounds after they were baked. Note the different ways Lindly and Cynthia recorded their discoveries—Cynthia with samples glued to the top of the embossing powder container, Lindly with pinches of samples baked together.

TECHNIQUE: DESIGNING THE SHAPES

1. Form a cane using steps 1, 2, and 4 from Folded Beads on page 60. Incorporate embossing powder in the blend for an interesting effect. Slice the cane and form the slices into petal shapes.

2. Create a tube of polymer by forming a cylinder, piercing the center with a double-pointed knitting needle, and adhering the "petals" in layers along the tube.

3. Form polymer rocks in various sizes and colors, following steps 1–4 from The Rocks on page 54. Flatten as desired and pierce with a needle tool.

Bringing It All Together

Lindly and Cynthia cured the beads and then evaluated what they had made. Was it enough for a bracelet? A necklace? Lindly suggested that if Cynthia would only make a few more beach stones in a particular shape or size it would make a particular group of beads they were evaluating really sing. After several rounds of discussing the need for "just a few more," they had amassed a significant pile of components, but still something was missing.

On the last working day, they both realized what their palette of subtle neutrals was missing—color. (Robert suggested stringing the beads with red waxed linen, which they tried but then dismissed as too bright.) Cynthia had noticed some tinted translucent pieces Seth was experimenting with and was intrigued. Where Seth was talking about water and waves, she saw an opportunity for adding color with "sea glass." Lindly thought this was a natural addition to the beach stones, adding precisely the color element and textural contrast they both wanted. She had a great feel for what colors could be mixed to replicate the glass. Cynthia quipped with a laugh, "I only wished that Lindly had studied beach stones that way!" Considering how much Cynthia and Lindly had discussed color at various points in the process, it was serendipitous that their piece came to life through their last-minute addition of sea glass.

LEFT: Accordion-folded cardstock keeps beads separated and cradled while they're baking. **BELOW:** Lindly had spent years collecting and examining sea glass from the Outer Banks, so fashioning these pieces came naturally.

"I learned to appreciate my skills—a basic and profound shift for me. Since I've loved rocks all my life, their shapes and colors come so easily to me that I didn't acknowledge the time and effort I had put into developing that skill. I understand their shapes in the same intuitive way that Lindly understands color."

—Cynthia

TECHNIQUE: CREATING A FINDING

1. Add dimension to individual pieces by making a finding from a straightened plastic-coated paper clip wrapped around a thin metal tube. Lindly and Cynthia had both seen Kathleen Amt use this technique years ago.

2. Embed the findings into the selected stones and folded lichen shapes. The plastic coating of the paper clip bonds to the polymer when cured, making a secure connection between the 2 materials.

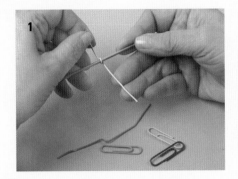

Making use of the paper-clip finding and the plethora of beads made during the week, Lindly and Cynthia created these bracelets, combing polymer rocks, lichen, and sea glass to complement the assembled necklace. Photograph by Richard K. Honaman Jr.

"I became more aware of my propensity to barge ahead into the making of the components before prototyping possibilities for finished pieces. Recently I have been auditioning components prior to production. I am pleased with this approach because I've found that little tweaks can greatly improve the stringing rhythm and design of the finished necklaces."

—*Lindly*

BE PASSIONATE ABOUT THE PROCESS
Dayle Doroshow and Sarah Shriver

When Dayle Doroshow and Sarah Shriver talk about themselves, it is interesting to note how similar they are—both in their process and their influences from the fiber arts. Sarah gathers source materials (fabric swatches, images of favorite paintings, and palettes) and then meditates on the pieces and the story they tell. Dayle embraces a similar process but collects the material and writes the "story" in her journal. Both of these artist-instructors are passionate about the process—the journey and exploration. However, their end results are quite different. Sarah produces hundreds of pieces, in her distinct style, to sell in high-end art shows each year. Dayle prefers to make only a few multiples of something she likes, and then she "imposes" a change to push her work in a different direction.

As longtime friends and admirers of each other's art, Dayle and Sarah knew a collaboration would be fruitful, but they also worried that their desire to find common ground might derail them. The process wasn't entirely smooth sailing; they were both so committed to working toward the other's style that their desire to accommodate each other bewildered them at times. Nonetheless, in pushing through the challenging moments, they created the one project in this book that is a true blending of their unique styles.

OPPOSITE/COLLABORATIVE PROJECT: Dayle Doroshow and Sarah Shriver, *Tribal Circus*, 2010; polymer, fiber, and leather cording; 3 x 18 x 1½ inches (7.5 x 45.5 x 3.8cm). Photograph by Richard K. Honaman Jr.

SHOWCASE DAYLE DOROSHOW

I became entranced with polymer, as did so many polymer artists, after reading *The New Clay: Techniques and Approaches to Jewelry Making* (Flower Valley Press, 1992) by Nan Roche. Once I had explored what Nan had to share, I took a workshop with Tory Hughes, which turned out to be life changing for me—as a person and as an artist. I left my full-time job and plunged headlong into making a living as an artist, and eventually also as a teacher.

My work is inspired by my love of history, faraway places, and ancient cultures. The styles fashioned by artisans of the past fuels my art and has led me to create my own modern-day "shards of history." That I am able to do this using a modern-day material—polymer—excites me creatively.

During the last two years I have thought deeply about personal voice and personal style, using a journal to document almost every aspect of this creative journey. The process allows me to work from stories that I discover or stories I write myself, and I'm moved by the depth and breadth of ideas that each story provides. The words suggest imagery, which then inspires shapes, surface designs, new forms, and a cornucopia of ideas to explore.

ABOVE: *Blooms*, 2010; polymer and fabric; 4 x 20 inches (10 x 51cm). Photograph by Dayle Doroshow. I am interested in exploring how these two mediums, polymer and fabric, can combine together—as I love the colors, pattern, and imagery possibilities of both.
RIGHT: *Butterfly Figure*, from the *Messengers and Storytellers* series, 2006; redwood, polymer, wire coil, hardware store parts, and feathers; 18 x 3½ x 3 inches (45.5 x 9 x 7.5cm). Photograph by Dayle Doroshow. I was playing with the idea of movement when I created this mixed-media figure. The "neck" is a large spring, covered by fibers and feathers, that allows the head to move when touched.

Ancient Memories, 2005; photographic emulsion transfer on polymer sculpture; 6 x 4 x 1 inches (15 x 10 x 2.5cm). Photograph by Dayle Doroshow. Inspired by the work of photographer Kathleen Carr, I took her process (used on paper) and developed a method for creating images on polymer. I am interested in exploring this way of making photographs three-dimensional.

Many of my influences relate to textiles—both in that the work is done through a lengthy process, thread by thread, and that those threads interconnect with each other to make something larger that is practical, cultural, and spiritual. The infinite variations of pattern inherent in the Kaleidoscope Caning process form a sort of visual language in number rhythms. Since nature is the source of all the number systems, I feel I am describing tiny facets of nature when I work.

Though I had been interested in textiles and other media for many years, it wasn't until I found polymer that I intuitively understood my artistic calling. I start each of my pieces with a drawing, knowing that I will need to translate the image into three dimensions when constructing it in polymer. When a line or dot is interpreted in polymer, it inevitably warps; I find that this adds something unique and unpredictable to the piece.

Turquoise Gold Collar, 2008; polymer, glass, amethyst, and brass beads; 1¼ x 20 inches (3 x 51cm). Photograph by George Post. Each bead fits together perfectly, allowing it to lie comfortably on the neck. The shine on the beads comes from a good deal of time spent with several grits of sandpaper and finally a trip to a jeweler's buffing wheel.

Acorn Necklace, 2010; polymer, carnelian, bone, and brass beads; 2 x 40 inches (5 x 101.5cm). Photograph by George Post. I wanted to create beads with more interesting shapes and larger in scale than I was accustomed to making. For this series, pollen and seed pods served as my inspiration.

Blue and Silver Necklace and Earrings, 2010; polymer, glass beads, sterling silver clasp and earwires; necklace: 1¼ x 20 inches (3 x 51cm); earrings: 1¼ x ¾ inches (3 x 2cm). Photograph by George Post. With this set I began using cores of Sculpey UltraLight and doing some fabrications in silver to accent the beads.

"Keeping a journal has allowed me to identify where I have been, where I am, and where I will be going. I find this approach pushes me to a new way of seeing and a new way of working."

Versailles Blooms Bracelet

Color can be a place to start working, show your individual voice, convey mood and emotion. I visited Versailles in 2008 and was propelled into creative high gear by the colors, patterns, and designs in the château—and especially by the spring flowers in the garden. I was thinking about the concept of personal voice and the importance of having a narrative, so I wrote some short vignettes that take place in the garden at Versailles in my journal.

Keeping a journal has allowed me to identify where I have been, where I am, and where I will be going. I find this approach pushes me to a new way of seeing and working. My sources provide a direction, a beginning, a point of departure, and allow me to take flight from something rather than nothing.

The jewelry design for this project began to emerge as a bracelet with flowers. To capture the abundance of gold at Versailles I added a metallic touch to the petals. This color is not a reflection of a real flower, of course, but rather was a creative choice inspired by the splendor at Versailles. The fleur-de-lis stamp is part of French history, decoratively and symbolically.

OPPOSITE: Dayle Doroshow, *Versailles Blooms*, 2011; polymer, fabric, and glass beads; 3 x 6 inches (7.5 x 15cm). Photograph by Richard K. Honaman Jr.

- polymer toolbox (see page 16)
- **polymer:** 2 oz. (57g) black; 1 oz. (28g) white; 1 oz. (28g) tan; 1 oz. (28g) each of 4 to 8 colors in a range of warm and cool tones (I used Fimo Soft for the black and white and Fimo Classic for the colors, as it has excellent tensile strength and receives texture and transfers well.)
- photocopies (toner-based) of two designs, one decorative and one reversed text
- texture plates and/or tools
- metallic powders
- carving tool
- circle template or cutter, ¾ inch (2cm) in diameter
- needle tool
- metallic composite leaf
- small piece of fiberfill
- measuring tool
- scissors
- small pieces of fabric that coordinate with your polymer (2)
- all-purpose cotton thread to match the fabric
- sewing needle
- sew-on Velcro, 1 inch (2.5cm) wide
- complementary or contrasting seed beads, size 8/0 (3)

BRACELET

1. Using the palette of your choice, create several blends following the instructions for a Multicolor Skinner Blend sheet on page 19. Roll them on a thin setting to approximately 5 x 3 inches (12.5 x 7.5cm). Using the stiff blade, cut the resulting sheets into 2 sections, each approximately 3 x 2½ inches (7.5 x 6.5cm), dividing them into lighter and darker hues.

   Thoroughly mix the white and tan polymer to create a light ivory color. Roll the ivory polymer through the pasta machine to create a relatively thin sheet; trim to 5 x 4 inches (12.5 x 10cm). Condition and roll out a sheet of black on a medium-thin setting on the pasta machine; trim to about 5 x 12 inches (12.5 x 30.5cm). The black sheet will be the backing polymer for all of the petals.

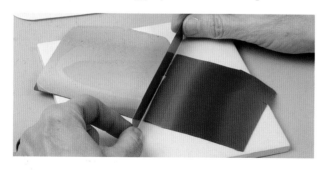

2. Place the decorative or text photocopies, toner-side down, onto a 2½ x 4–inch (6.5 x 10cm) section of the ivory polymer sheet. Burnish the paper securely to the polymer using your finger, and then set the assembly aside for at least 30 minutes. Slowly peel the papers off. The toner,

now on the polymer, will be slightly sticky and wet, so avoid touching it. Carefully layer the ivory polymer onto a 2½ x 4–inch (6.5 x 10cm) section of the black polymer sheet. Roll these assemblies through the pasta machine on a medium-thin setting; this will elongate and stretch the photocopy design, which adds a painterly look.

NOTE: All of the sheets created for making petals for the flowers in this bracelet are rolled to the same medium-thin setting on the pasta machine.

3. Cut a 2½ x 5–inch (6.5 x 12.5cm) section from the black polymer sheet. Press rubber stamps, texture plates, or your favorite personal texture designs onto the sheet. Using your finger, dust metallic powder on only the raised areas of the impressed design. Use only a little powder and dust lightly, making several passes. Roll the textured sheet through the pasta machine on a medium-thin setting, flattening and stretching the design, but still retaining the metallic pattern. Layer the textured sheet onto a 3½ x 5–inch (9 x 12.5cm) section of the remaining black polymer sheet and

roll through the pasta machine on a medium-thin setting Set aside. Thoroughly clean the pasta machine.

4. Layer a lighter section of the Skinner Blend sheet onto a 2 2½ x 5–inch (6.5 x 12.5cm) section of the remaining black polymer sheet. Using a carving tool, make simple small nicks and gouges through the top layer (the blend) on one half of the sheet to reveal the black polymer below. Leave the other half untouched. Roll this sheet through the pasta machine on a medium-thin setting. This will flatten the carvings and spread the design but allow it to retain the effect.

Repeat the process, layering a darker section of the Skinner Blend sheet onto the remaining 2½ x 4–inch (6.5 x 10cm) ivory polymer sheet, carving to reveal the ivory polymer below and rolling through the pasta machine at a medium-thin setting.

NOTE: Create tools like Dayle's by covering handles with scrap polymer and then covering the scrap with canes or decorative touches of your choice.

5. Using an X-Acto knife or craft blade, and working freehand or using a paper template, cut petals from the different sheets of polymer created in steps 2–4. Cut as many petals as possible. Each finished flower has 5 petals, and when assembling you will want a large assortment to choose from. Begin to assemble the petals into flowers.

6. Assess your progress. Create more petals to fill in where you feel something is missing. Maybe a collaged petal, created from assembling leftover pieces from each of the other petals, or a plain petal with small dots added will work.

7. Cut a ¾-inch- (2cm-) diameter circle of polymer from the remaining pieces of a black or decorated sheet. Transfer the assembled petals onto the circle base, overlapping as necessary. Using a needle tool, poke 3 holes in the center of the flower, going through the base circle. These holes will be used to sew the blooms securely onto the bracelet band. Repeat to create 3 blooms.

8. Make several small, approximately ⅜-inch (9mm) shaped beads out of ivory, black with gold leaf, and blended scraps. These will be used for the centers of the blooms. Using a needle tool, poke a hole in the center of each of these little beads.

9. Cure the blooms face down over a small pile of fiberfill so that they have a three-dimensional shape. Cure according to manufacturer's instructions, and allow them to cool to room temperature.

10. Measure the circumference of your wrist and add 2 inches (5cm). Cut 2 pieces of coordinating fabric to 1½ inches (3.8cm) x the determined length. With right sides together and using a ¼-inch (6mm) seam allowance, sew 3 sides—both long sides and 1 short side—closed. Clip the seams, and then turn the pocket of fabric inside out. Turn under the raw edges of the remaining short side and hand-sew it closed. For the closure, sew a piece of Velcro on one side of one end and the other side of the other, allowing the two ends to overlap once fastened.

11. Sew through the center of the bracelet and through the holes of one flower to connect them together. Sew through the fabric and flower at least two times. Do not cut the thread. String on 2 or 3 polymer beads (made in step 8) and 1 seed bead. Pass the needle back down through the polymer beads, the flower, and the fabric (skipping the seed bead, which acts as a "stop" to hold down the polymer beads) to secure them all together. Secure the thread and cut. Repeat two times, placing a bloom on the left and the right of the center bloom.

REFINING AND EDITING IDEAS

Step back for a period of time (it could be fifteen minutes, a day, or one week) and examine what's working and what's not. Break down the elements, identify the best qualities, edit out the superfluous ones. I consult with supportive artist friends who help me see things I couldn't.

There may be a design element that just doesn't work in a piece, but rather than trashing the whole piece, brainstorm and find another way to cover, cut out, replace, overlay, carve into, and so forth. Nine times out of ten the new design is even better than the original concept.

"Other artists can be a tremendous resource. . . . The braided fabric that Frida Kahlo wore in her hair inspired this particular design. Blues and greens from a Van Gogh painting offered the uplifting colors of spring."

Braided Bracelet

Other artists can be a tremendous resource. The color decisions made by my favorite painters are all there on the canvas for me to see. Sometimes I will single out a particular relationship of several colors used in a painting and then work with my colored pencils until I have built up a palette. Or, in a less literal way, I might consider the way an artist has lived as an inspiration. The braided fabric that Frida Kahlo wore in her hair inspired this particular design. Blues and greens from a Van Gogh painting offered the uplifting colors of spring.

SUPPLIES

- polymer toolbox (see page 16)
- **polymer:** 4 oz. (113.5g) white; 3 oz. (85g) dark purple; 3 oz. (85g) blue; 3 oz. (85g) turquoise; 3 oz. (85g) light yellow; 3 oz. (85g) ivory; 2 oz. (57g) of scrap; less than 2 oz. (57g) black; less than 1 oz. (28g) green; less than 1 oz. (28g) orange (I used Fimo Classic, for its colors, texture, and ease of baking.)
- cardstock
- pencil
- scissors
- tape measure
- variable-speed or handheld drill
- drill bit, #70
- cyanoacrylate glue (e.g., Super Glue)
- round elastic cord
- beading needle, #10
- Nymo thread

PREVIOUS PAGE: Sarah Shriver, *Braided Bracelet*, 2011; polymer and elastic cord; 1½ x 7 inches (3.8 x 18cm). Photograph by Richard K. Honaman Jr.

BRACELET

1. Use the colors listed or choose your own palette with at least two basic colors—one for the braid and one for the background. (Using water-soluble colored pencils, I made sketches to fine-tune and flesh out the color scheme for my cane, as shown opposite, below.) Keep in mind that adjacent colors on a color wheel are always relative to one another, so you must consider how they work together. Remember to include white and ivory for tints and black for shades. The illusion of the braid's three-dimensional in-and-out weave is accomplished by using blends with dark ends to imply shadows and light ends to imply highlights. The instructions that follow reference purple/blue for the braid and turquoise/green for the background; however, any colors can be selected.

   TIP: Use a larger amount of polymer than you need for one bracelet because you will find it easier to control, and you will have more cane to experiment with different-shaped beads.

2. Following the instructions for Controlling the Skinner Blend on page 19, create 8 blended sheets, each approximately 3½ x 3½ inches (9 x 9cm), rolled through the thickest setting on the machine—4 blend variations in purple/blue and 4 in turquoise/green.

   Beginning with the blends for the braid, roll out each of the 4 purple/blue sheets to a medium thickness on the pasta machine and cut each in half so you now have 8 smaller sheets.

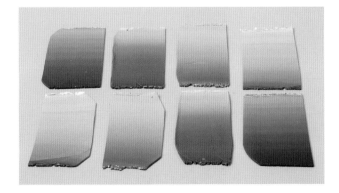

3. To create a bull's-eye cane "inclusion" shown in Step 4, roll an orange snake. Roll out a sheet of purple on a medium thickness. Begin to wrap the snake with the purple sheet and stop just as the purple begins to overlap itself. Using a stiff blade, cut the purple sheet at the line of demarcation.

Wrap the purple around the snake and seal the seam, forming a smooth tube.

TIP: You can use these details to emphasize the light side of the blend by adding lighter colors or the dark side by doing the reverse. This is a very free process, and it's fine to get carried away as long as you do not add so much light to the dark or dark to the light that you confuse which side is the "shadow."

4. Stack the pieces of the purple/blue sheets, adding inclusions—or not—as you go. Arrange the layers so there is interest and color differences from the blends, and keep the lighter sections on the same end. If adding inclusions, be sure they are arranged through the layer. Compress the layers, squeezing out any trapped air pockets.

5. Reduce the stack by pushing the dark side toward the light side. This can be confusing, so stop and ask yourself if the ends you are pushing on are dark all the way across and light all the way across. Utilize the techniques listed in Technique: Elongating a Block, page 83. Keep going until the "face" of the cane is approximately ¾ x 1½ inches (2 x 3.8cm); the exact length is determined by the amount of clay used.

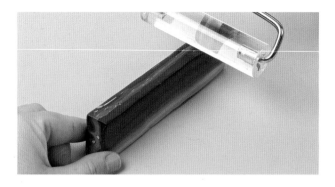

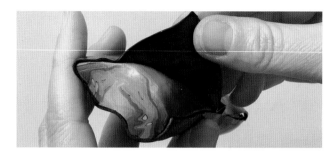

6. Measure the length of your cane and cut it in half. Put the two light sides together, facing one another.

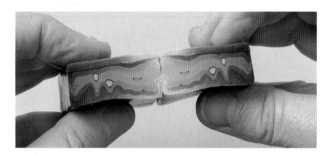

9. Cut the cane into 4 pieces, and puzzle them together, forming a braid.

7. A template will help you shape your pieces correctly. Examine the template shown below and replicate the shape on a piece of cardstock, keeping in mind the dimensions should suit the face of the cane created in step 6. Cut out the template, trace around it, and cut out the tracing to create 2 templates.

10. Cut the extending bits off one end of the cane. Add the cut-off sections to the corresponding spot on the opposite end, making it so that the cane has two flat ends to push against for reducing.

Place a template on each end of the cane, making sure they are oriented in the same direction. Keep pinching and pulling your cane until the shape matches the templates. Let the cane elongate as necessary.

8. Using a dark piece of polymer in the hue of the cane (in this case, dark purple), wrap the concave/inside curve and one end of the cane; this will add to the graphic illusion, exaggerating the shadow. Then put a very thin sheet of black around the other end and the convex/outside of the cane.

TIP: The braid is a tessellated (repeatable) form, so you can cut the extending shapes from one side and add them back to the other side without disturbing the continuity of the pattern.

11. Lay the braid on a piece of cardstock. Trace the outline. Cut off the sides of the paper straight with the width of the braid. Cut along the outline and discard the shape that mirrors the braid, leaving curved templates that will be used to cut the cane in step 12.

12. Build and reduce a turquoise/green stack following steps 2, 4, and 5. Measure and cut the stack in half, matching the longer side, while keeping the lighter colors together as well as the darker. This stack needs to be the same size as the braid cane; you may need to manipulate the shape of the block to achieve that.

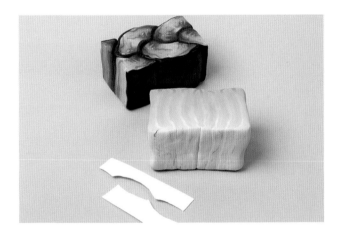

13. Cut the turquoise/green stack exactly in half, creating a lighter and darker stack. Place a template onto one of the halves. Bend a tissue blade and carefully cut the cane to match template. Adjust as necessary so this stack matches the braid. Repeat with the other half.

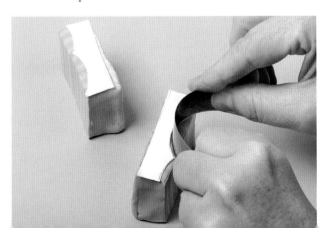

14. Assemble the pieces of the cane, making sure the points of the background pieces fit tightly into the valleys of the braid pieces.

15. Reduce the cane as described in step 5 to approximately 1 x 1 inch (2.5 x 2.5cm) and then cutting it in half. Store one-half and reduce the other half to about ³/₄ x ³/₄ inch (2 x 2cm) to use for this first bracelet.

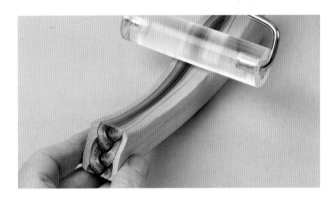

| ELONGATING A BLOCK |

The following simple tips can be used to elongate a block as much as necessary.

- Keep close to your work surface, and use it to impose flat sides on your stack as you reduce.
- Go back and forth between your hands and the work surface.
- Stretch the cane using your hands and/or an acrylic brayer.

16. Cut the cane in half; then stack the two halves next to each other, mirroring the image lengthwise.

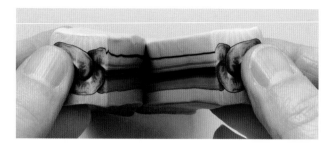

17. Reduce the cane until it measures approximately 1 x ½ inch (2.5cm x 13mm). Cut a pair of slices (approximately ¹⁄₁₆-inch [1.5mm] thick or less) for the veneer of your first bead. Put the slices next to each other on the table and push the seam together a bit so they are stuck to one another.

18. Roll out a tube of scrap polymer to a diameter of about ³⁄₈ inch (9mm). Wrap the two slices of veneer around the tube. It's best if there is a little gap between the edges of the veneered pieces, so cut out a V shape in the scrap polymer tube. Compress the bead so the veneer edges meet perfectly.

19. Pinch the ends of the bead closed—one side at a time. Really pay attention to the shape. I like to flatten mine or pinch the center in for a kind of peanut shape; use your imagination. Check the size of the bead. Is it a size you would wear? If not, adjust the pieces until it seems right

for you. Measure your wrist and mark a piece of paper with the length. Make as many beads as necessary to fit your wrist. Cure according to manufacturer's instructions.

20. After the beads are cured and cooled, drill a hole through the center of each bead using a variable-speed or other handheld drill. (I used a Dremel drill suspended in a drill press so the drill bit would pass through the bead straight.) Bring the bead up toward the drill bit and push it into the bead, working until just over halfway through. Flip the bead and drill to just over halfway until the holes meet in the middle. Repeat for all of the beads except one.

21. For the final bead, drill the same way, but enlarge the hole so it is a bit bigger than the others—this will allow you to hide the closure inside. Apply a dab of cyanoacrylate glue to one end of your round elastic cord. Let the glue dry so the end is stiff and easier to pass through the beads. String all of your bracelet beads, making sure you start or stop at the bead with the larger hole. Thread a beading needle with a length of Nymo thread. With the elastic cord under slight tension, stitch the two ends of the cord together. Cut the ends clean, and then pull the join of the cord into the large hole so that it is well hidden.

COLLABORATIVE PROJECT

Tribal Circus

Dayle and Sarah were eager to work together. They were the only team to meet in person and lay a lot of groundwork prior to the gathering at the Outer Banks. The general concept established at that early stage included using large forms that they would create with Sculpey UltraLight, possibly incorporating fiber and metal, and the understanding that the piece would be jewelry. They also formulated a palette—or so they thought.

Navigating Misunderstandings

The team's initial face-to-face meeting in Dayle's home was tremendously productive. They established general ideas about how they would proceed, sketched out their palette, and set a date by which they would each mail partially made beads to each other. The collaboration began so smoothly that Sarah was shocked when she opened the envelope with Dayle's beads to find a completely different take on the palette she thought they had agreed on. They each "saw" different colors, even though they were working from the same sketches.

Finding Common Ground

Upon arrival in North Carolina, Dayle and Sarah invited the input of others, and positioned their workspaces in the midst of the hustle and bustle of the main room of the house. They welcomed the addition of Lindly and Cynthia to the table and were open to discussions from most everyone in the house. Having the ocean just over their shoulders didn't hurt either.

The pair struggled in the beginning, each trying to be sensitive to the other's style: Sarah, orderly and refined; Dayle, organic and loose. They were both working out of their comfort zones and saw this push and pull as part of the challenge of working on a collaborative project.

The team had already decided that they would work with UltraLight, a relatively new product, so they decided to focus on this shared desire. The two explored making larger forms that would remain lightweight. They discovered that after curing, the beads had a similar feel to balsa wood and were easy to carve and sand.

Sarah and Dayle made decisions about their palette using water-soluble pencils and bead sketches.

"I think my favorite part in this process was when we mailed our ideas back and forth. I felt the elements of surprise and lightheartedness and the ability to spin off of Dayle's ideas, but I could respond in my own time from my own more comfortable place of solitude."

—*Sarah*

Trying to Embrace the Process

Dayle and Sarah continued to work—sometimes together with challenging discussions, and sometimes apart. They each created sheets of polymer in their palette to be used as veneers, sometimes using the techniques showcased in their individual projects. For instance, Dayle used carved Skinner Blend sheets (see step 4 of Bracelet on page 81) and smooth sheets of scrap polymer. Sarah made simple canes similar to those created in step 12 of Bracelet on page 83; she even tried, for the first time, an extruded cane.

Both Dayle and Sarah thought a particular accordion-shaped bead was interesting. However, they struggled when trying to flesh out the concept, finding these beads particularly time-consuming to make. Initially, they built the beads by making rough disks of UltraLight, pinching a few of these plump forms together and curing them. They then applied veneers using multiple steps. First, they affixed a thin sheet of color to either the interior crevasse or the exterior pointed edge. Next, using thin sheets of a contrasting color, they applied a second veneer to the remaining exposed area. They used rubber burnishers and clay shapers to wedge and smooth the polymer around the form, curing the beads after each layer of veneer was positioned.

After they had made five or six beads, Cynthia pointed out that if they formed and applied the veneer to each disk separately and then put the disks together for the final baking, the process would be much easier. Dayle responded, with a laugh, that Cynthia "could have told them that sooner," and Sarah added that they would never make those beads again!

Dayle and Sarah took time between making individual beads to evaluate their growing pile. The first few days produced lots of beads but no agreement as to how to proceed with what might become the final piece.

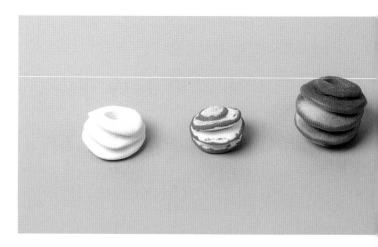

TOP: At first, Dayle and Sarah fashioned their accordion-shaped beads and then applied the veneers. They found the process to be extremely tedious.
ABOVE: Having observed their struggles, Cynthia offered some guidance. Simply changing the sequence of the steps made the process much easier.

"The journey itself was mostly a joy—lots of laughter, brainstorming possibilities, ups and downs, things not turning out as expected, sometimes a disaster becoming a 'beauty.' The creative journey itself was the important part for me. What I learned from our collaboration was an appreciation (and enjoyment) of taking more time to 'finish' a piece, more time to think about possibilities—not just the obvious first one—and allowing my hands, heart, and mind to work more fully together."

—Dayle

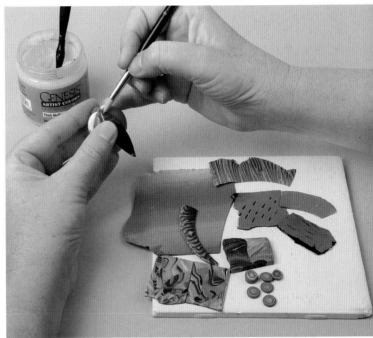

ABOVE: UltraLight can be sculpted in any shape (as in the two long beads), pulled from a mold (as in the two flower-shaped beads), or carved and sanded into a more refined shape, as Dayle is doing here. **RIGHT:** Dayle applied Genesis thick medium to the area prior to attaching a veneer. This viscous medium cures along with the polymer and has a nonslip characteristic that offers good control when applying the veneers.

Inviting Outside Feedback

Midweek, Dayle and Sarah gathered all the finished, partially finished, and unadorned UltraLight beads and scraps of veneers, and requested a consultation with Jeff. They were having difficulty coming to a decision about what might make the perfect end product or project. He advised them to separate the beads into piles of their least and most promising forms, and to continue to work for that "just-in-case, aha bead" that could emerge.

That evening, before Dayle drifted off to sleep, she made a mental note to tell Sarah the next day that she thought they needed a mustard-colored bead to set off the rest of the beads, which were olive greens and reds. When Dayle arrived at the worktable early the next morning she found a bead—in that exact mustard color—with a note from Sarah, asking if she liked it. The idea of possible ESP sent the team into a renewed work mode.

"Process, and the journey that ensues, are the common thread for Dayle and Sarah, even though their work styles are very different. Their friendship and mutual respect for each other added a layer of complexity to the process. Their tenacity and love of the journey kept them moving forward to ultimately yield a truly blended body of work."

—Jeff

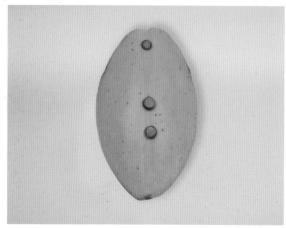

ABOVE: Dayle and Sarah shifted gears midweek and began to focus on creating a finished piece. Would it be a series of brooches, a long necklace with all the beads, or perhaps a series of single pendants? Jeff consulted with the team.

Celebrating a Shared Passion

Dayle and Sarah decided to introduce fiber into some of the beads. They each had brought with them a variety of their favorite fringes, yarns, threads, and other accents from their collections. They were both excited to incorporate something they were passionate about.

Traveling a Path Together

At the end of the week, Dayle and Sarah evaluated all the beads they had made, and, independently, each selected their favorites and created a mock-up. Again, they invited input from Jeff, and this time they had Cynthia and Lindly listen in this time as well. They found that they had a few beads in common, so they decided to start with those beads. The decision on how to string the necklaces was serendipitous— Jeff offered some leather he had brought with him, and they agreed that it was exactly the right material to finish off their "tribal" necklaces.

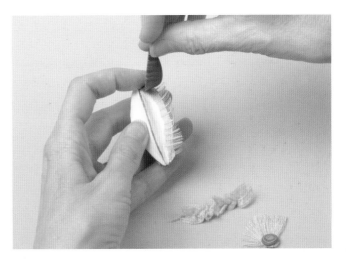

FAR LEFT: Sometimes collaborations occur without words. Sarah, a night owl, stayed up late making this mustard-colored bead, not knowing that it was exactly the thing on Dayle's mind at that very moment. **TOP:** Dayle applied fringed fabric with Genesis Thick Medium, an extender, and then added veneers, covering sections of the beads and the edges of the fabric. **ABOVE:** Sarah and Dayle both brought a stash of fibers for possible inclusion on the beads. Hitting on the same idea, Sarah added a tuft of threads at one end of a bead (left), while Dayle created a circle of fiber fringe to embellish a snail-shaped bead (right). **LEFT:** After Lindly noticed the team had created several colorways in their beads, Dayle and Sarah actually created three separate necklaces. Photographs by Richard K. Honaman Jr.

USE NEW MEDIUMS
Seth Lee Savarick and Robert Dancik

Robert, primarily a metalsmith who uses polymer mostly as a tool to inform his work, was frankly intimidated to work with Seth, whose polymer work he so admired. Seth, on the other hand, viewed the metalwork he had done in the past as strictly structural. He was excited to work with Robert, as it would push him to use metal as an integral design element. Respect for each other's strengths was a salient feature of their pairing—as was their willingness to explore a medium very different from their own.

Seth believes his best work comes from having a clear, thought-out vision that evolves over time, as he works and reworks individual pieces until they are something he is ready to share. Robert, like Seth, works well within the limits of assignments, but they are generally assignments he gives himself. Both men were confident in their abilities to be capable collaborators, and they were correct. Seth's knowledge of metal from fabrication and casting classes allowed the two to establish an easy and comfortable relationship—he understood Robert's "language," yet was content deferring to his expertise with the material. Likewise, because Robert doesn't see himself as a polymer artist, it was easy for him to accede to Seth on those decisions. Their knowledge of and regard for the other's primary medium gave them critical distance, dispelling any competitiveness that might have naturally occurred in the collaboration.

OPPOSITE/COLLABORATIVE PROJECT: Seth Lee Savarick and Robert Dancik, *Boats with Gossamer Waves*, 2011; polymer and sterling silver; each boat: 2¼ x ⅜ x ½ inches (5.5 x 0.9 x 1.3cm); necklace: 22⅝ inches (57.5cm) long. Photograph by Richard K. Honaman Jr.

I was first introduced to polymer in 1993 through the book arts of Kathleen Amt. Shortly thereafter I began working with polymer as a creative outlet to augment my work as a printmaker and graphic artist. I had always been drawn to working in three dimensions, and polymer seemed like the perfect medium to further explore the integration of form, color, and design. After working with polymer for a few years, I put it away to pursue other endeavors.

In 2001 I found myself drawn to polymer again, and I have been focused on working with polymer as a fine-art medium ever since. My early work with polymer developed out of an interest in the Japanese inro form and fine lacquer work. Designed to hang from the kimono sash and to carry small items when garments did not have pockets, these small vessels resonated with me. Looking back, I believe that a big part of the attraction was the scale of the pieces. I really wanted my work to be functional, worn, seen, and used.

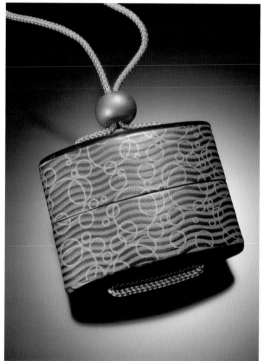

ABOVE: *Water Inro*, 2004; polymer, liquid polymer, acrylic paint, and silk cord; inro: 2¾ x 3½ x ¾ inches (7 x 9 x 2cm); cord: 24 inches (61cm). Photograph by Robert Diamante. The surface design came from the idea that water forms both bubbles and waves.

LEFT: *Green Inro*, 2004; polymer, acrylic paint, liquid polymer, 18K gold powder, acrylic medium, and silk cord; inro: 5 x 3 x ¾ inches (12.5 x 7. x 2cm); cord: 32 inches (81cm). Photograph by Robert Diamante. The surface pattern was created by playing with a stylized font using the letters *E* and *G*.

Hockney Inro, 2004; polymer, liquid polymer, acrylic paint, and silk cord; inro: 3 x 3½ x ¾ inches (7.5 x 9 x 2cm); cord: 24 inches (61cm). Photograph by Robert Diamante. The inspiration for this inro came after seeing a production of the opera *Die Frau ohne Schatten*, with sets designed by artist David Hockney.

SHOWCASE ROBERT DANCIK

Teaching art has always kept me not only in a creative mode but also on the forefront of exploration with new materials. I have had the advantage of working and playing with unusual materials, bringing them across channels as art forms. For instance, concrete from my sculptures has crept into my jewelry forms.

Because polymer has no real historical or material references, it helps me express my ideas without imposing its will or references on my work. By contrast, a material like gold has numerous varied references—it's royal, rare, and precious; if I use gold in a piece, viewers automatically make these connections. I can use polymer to establish texture, pattern, color, contrast, and so forth. These "layers of visual information" convey meaning. This doesn't ensure that the viewer will exactly get what I am trying to say, but it does allow me, as the maker, to incorporate only the references I desire.

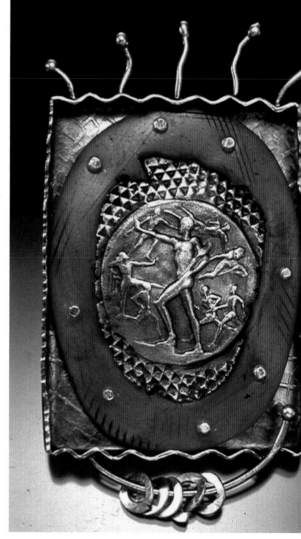

ABOVE: *Kewpies and Marilyn*, 2008–2010; polymer, photo transfers, sterling, cubic zirconia, pearls, turquoise, and carnelian; dimensions variable. Photograph by Douglas Foulke. This work is from a series of pieces I made about various American icons.

RIGHT: *Run/Jump/Fly*, 2008; polymer, sterling silver, and fine silver (metal clay); 2¾ x 1⅝ x ¼ inches (7 x 4 x 0.6cm). Photograph by Douglas Foulke. This piece is a whimsical look at a serious Olympic medallion I made a cast of during the summer Olympics.

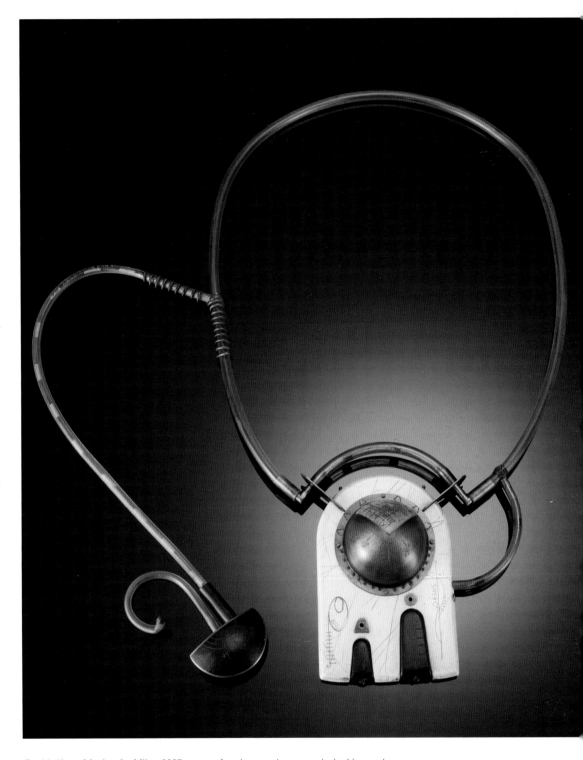

Double Heart Monitor for Milan, 2007; copper, faux bone, polymer, surgical tubing, and brass; 23 x 15 x 1 inches (58.5 x 38 x 2.5cm). Photograph by Douglas Foulke. My father died of a heart attack when I was fairly young. This was one of several pieces I made with the thought that if, at the time, he had been wearing such a monitor for his heart, his demise may have been averted.

"When I first began to explore jewelry forms I quickly found that the work being done by most jewelry artists was far smaller than the scale at which I felt most comfortable working. This chunk bead celebrates what I like to call 'my working scale.'"

Chunk Bead

The chunk bead, as I like to call it, utilizes a hollow-form construction technique that gives the bead its terrific volume yet keeps it lightweight. Fabricating three-dimensional geometric shapes requires precise craftsmanship. To achieve superior results, take your time and practice. Eventually, your chunk beads will become wonderful jewelry pieces.

When I first began to explore jewelry forms I quickly found that the work being done by most jewelry artists was far smaller than the scale at which I felt most comfortable working. This chunk bead celebrates what I like to call "my working scale." Once you master the basic construction, however, you can make these beads at any scale, large or small. You can also play with the dimensions of the face of the bead, as well as the depth of the curve.

Chunk beads make a great canvas for showcasing virtually any polymer technique. In this project, screen printing is used as the surface treatment. However, you could use anything you'd like, including caning, *mokume gane*, and ikat techniques—all of which can be found within the pages of this book.

OPPOSITE: Seth Lee Savarick, *Chunk Bead*, 2011; polymer, acrylic paint, and stainless steel cable; chunk bead: 2⅝ x 2⅞ x 1 inches (6.7 x 7.3 x 2.5cm): cable: 20½ inches (52cm). Photograph by Richard K. Honaman Jr.

SUPPLIES

- polymer toolbox (see page 16)
- **polymer:** 3 oz. (85g) scrap (or black); 2 oz. (57g) black; 2 oz. (57g) metallic gold; 2 oz. (57g) peacock pearl (I used Premo! for this project, on account of its strength; Fimo or Kato Polyclay could be used as well.)
- steel ruler, 6-inch (15cm)
- box cutter
- cardboard mailing tube, 2½-inch (6.5cm) diameter
- 8 x 8–grid graph paper, 8½ x 11 inches (21.5 x 28cm)
- masking tape
- X-Acto knife, fitted with #11 blade
- cardstock, 8½ x 11 inches (21.5 x 28cm)
- copy paper
- wet/dry sandpaper, 220- and 400-grit
- acid-free, smooth matte board, 3 x 5 inches (7.5 x 12.5cm)

- Translucent Liquid Sculpey (TLS)
- paintbrush, dedicated to TLS
- scissors
- ballpoint pen
- variable-speed or hand drill
- drill bits, #44 and #50
- paper towels
- waxed paper
- screen-printing stencils
- palette knife
- Golden Heavy Body Acrylic: iridescent bright gold (fine); iridescent pearl (fine); quinacridone red; nickle azo gold; diarylide yellow; interference violet (fine); and phthalo blue (red shade)
- small squeegee or old credit card
- small ball stylus
- fine-tipped paintbrush, dedicated to sizing
- gold-leaf size

- small container of water
- 18K gold or composite gold leaf
- gilder's brush
- soft, lint-free cloth
- cable necklace with clasp, 16-inch (40.5cm)

Optional (for making a sanding tile)
- scissors
- wet/dry sandpaper, 220-grit
- double-sided adhesive sheets
- smooth glazed ceramic tile, 6 x 6 inches (15 x 15cm)
- Follow the directions that come with the screen stencil film to create your own designs or use purchased screen-printing stencils. See Resources on page 156 for more information.

CHUNK BEAD

1. Working from the factory edge, measure and, using a box cutter, cut a 5-inch (12.5cm) section off of a mailing tube. Cut a 5 x 9–inch (12.5 x 23cm) strip of graph paper. Wrap the strip tightly around the cut length of tube, using the factory edge and the graph lines to keep the paper square. Tape the seam down with masking tape. The paper should fit snuggly and not move on the tube.

   TIP: Rub the graph paper with a lump of scrap polymer. This will leave some residue, which will help the polymer adhere.

2. Using a metal ruler and an X-Acto knife, cut a 3 x 2¾– inch (7.5 x 7cm) rectangular template from heavy cardstock. Set it aside. Condition a chunk of scrap polymer; roll it on the thickest setting of the pasta machine into a 4 x 4–inch (10 x 10cm) sheet; then lay it onto a sheet of copy paper. Place the template onto the polymer sheet. Holding the stiff blade perpendicular to the work surface, to ensure perfectly vertical cuts (like a guillotine), cut around the template. Remove excess polymer.

3. Lift the polymer from the copy paper, and (avoiding the seam and masking tape on the tube so you don't get bumps in the polymer) gently lay the polymer onto the graph paper with the 3-inch (7.5cm) edges of the polymer running around the tube. Use the graph paper lines as a guide to keep things square. Place a few small pieces of scrap polymer onto a ceramic tile; then place the tube between the scrap polymer pieces, stabilizing the tube. Cure according to manufacturer's instructions. Allow the piece to cool completely.

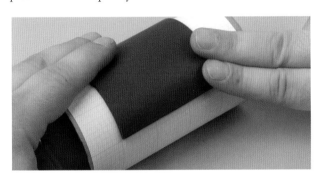

4. Remove the cured polymer from the tube—it is the beginning of your bead core. Use 220-grit sandpaper or a sanding tile (see Making a Sanding Tile, above right) and water to wet-sand the ends of the bead core flat.

Roll a 4 x 4–inch (10 x 10cm) sheet of scrap polymer on the thickest setting of the pasta machine; then cut it in half, forming two 4 x 2–inch (10 x 5cm) rectangles. Place one rectangle on the matte board and cover with a sheet of copy paper. Use your fingers and a small square of heavy cardstock to gently burnish the raw polymer rectangle to the matte board. Remove the copy paper.

MAKING A SANDING TILE

1. Using scissors, cut a 5 x 5–inch (12.5 x 12.5cm) square of 220-grit wet/dry sandpaper. Peel off one side of an adhesive sheet to expose the adhesive. Firmly adhere the smooth side of the sandpaper to the adhesive sheet and cut away the excess that extends beyond the sandpaper.

2. Peel and expose the other side of the adhesive tape and smoothly adhere the sandpaper to a 6 x 6–inch (15 x 15cm) glazed tile. You will find many uses for this flat sanding tile, and you may make them in other grits; they are a great addition to your toolbox. The sanding tile is shown on page 100.

5. Paint a thin coat of Translucent Liquid Sculpey (TLS) onto one end of the bead core and press gently onto the polymer rectangle on the matte board. Set the piece aside for 10 minutes, allowing a bond to form. Trim the sheet to the curve of the bead core, keeping the stiff blade straight as you make many cuts, like a guillotine. Make a final straight cut across the open back side of the bead face. Paint a thin coat of TLS along the interior joint where the sides meet the raw bead-core end. Place on a ceramic tile and cure. Allow the bead core to cool completely, and gently remove it from the matte board.

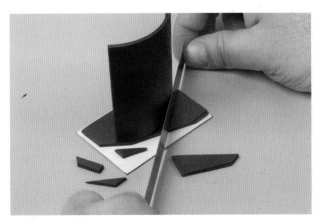

6. Repeat steps 4 and 5 to form the other end of the bead core, and then use 200-grit sandpaper to wet-sand the edges of the bead core to ensure they are flat.

7. Place the bead, half-round side down, on a sheet of copy paper. Trace around the bead end, and cut it out with scissors. Securely position the template on one end of the bead. Determine where you want the stringing hole to be (toward the back and top is best, so it doesn't flip forward when worn), and mark with a pen. Use a drill fitted with a #44 drill bit to create a small hole. Flip the template over and place it onto the other end of the bead. Be careful to align the holes directly across from one another, so your bead will hang straight. Make the second hole.

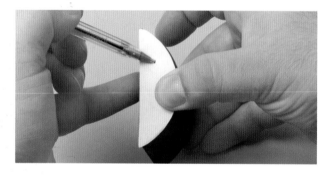

NOTE: Once the back is in place, the holes will allow air to escape while the bead is being cured.

8. Roll a 4 x 4–inch (10 x 10cm) sheet of black polymer on the thickest setting of the pasta machine and burnish to the matte board as in step 4. Paint a thin coat of TLS on the back edges of the bead core, press down gently onto the sheet of raw polymer, and allow it to sit for 10 minutes. Trim the sheet to each side of the bead core using a stiff blade. Remove the excess polymer from the matte board, and then place the matte board onto a ceramic tile; cure. Allow the bead core to cool completely; then remove it from the matte board.

Wet-sand the bead core smooth. Sand the front and side surfaces with 400-grit wet/dry sandpaper so all edges are flush and square, and all surfaces are smooth. Do not sand the back surface. Thoroughly dry the bead with a paper towel. Your hollow chunk-bead core is now done and ready for the screen-printed veneers.

SIDE VENEER

1. Roll a 6 x 4–inch (15 x 10cm) sheet of metallic gold polymer to a medium-thick setting on the pasta machine, and place it on an 8 x 12–inch (20.5 x 30.5cm) piece of waxed paper. Place the screen stencil, shiny side down, onto the polymer sheet. Using a palette knife, apply a 1/4-inch- (6mm-) thick line of iridescent bright gold (fine) paint across the top of the screen.

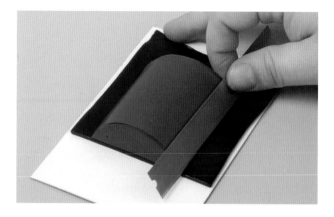

2. Place the squeegee at a 45-degree angle to the polymer sheet, just above the paint, yet still on the screen. Using light pressure and keeping the squeegee at a 45-degree angle, draw the squeegee down to the bottom of the screen so that the open areas of the screen are well filled. It takes

very little pressure to push the paint through the screen. Immediately peel the screen up and off the polymer sheet. Wash the paint from the screen in gently running cold water. Blot the screen, and then hang it up to air dry.

3. When the paint is completely dry (about 15 minutes), cut the printed sheet in half to form two 3 x 4–inch (7.5 x 10cm) veneer sheets. Place one veneer, printed side down, onto a small sheet of waxed paper. Lightly coat one of the ends of the bead core with TLS, making sure not to fill the drill hole. Use the waxed paper to transfer the veneer to the bead core. Smooth the polymer to be sure that you do not trap any air. Trim the veneer flush to the edge of the bead core. Remove the waxed paper. Gently press a mark into the veneer where the drill hole is. Use the ball stylus to deepen the depression and stretch the polymer, but do not punch through. Place the bead core onto a ceramic tile, cure, and allow to cool completely.

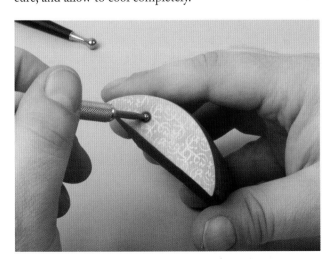

Repeat the process with the second veneer sheet for the other end of the bead. Carefully sand the veneer edges with 400-grit wet/dry sandpaper so they are flush with the face and back of the bead core. Be careful not to sand the printed surface of the veneer. Using a drill and a #44 drill bit, redrill the holes at the marks on both sides of the bead.

FACE VENEER

1. Roll a 6 x 6–inch (15 x 15cm) sheet of peacock pearl polymer to a medium-thick setting on the pasta machine and place on waxed paper. Screen print as in steps 1 and 2 of the Side Veneer section on page 100, using a blend of paints in your favorite colors. You may choose to print additional layers in varying colors to add depth to the design. Be sure to allow the paint to dry completely between each layer and before applying the printed polymer to the bead core.

The design in the image below was created in 4 layers, as detailed in Visualizing the Layers, page 102.

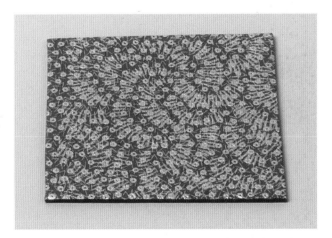

2. Cut out and lay a 4 x 4–inch (10 x 10cm) cardstock template over your favorite part of the stenciled sheet and trim. Cut the 4 x 4–inch (10 x 10cm) square into 3 or 4 interestingly shaped pieces.

Paint a thin coat of TLS onto the face of the bead core. Arrange the printed veneer pieces on the bead core, leaving small gaps to create the illusion that the veneer has been shattered. Use a piece of waxed paper to smooth the sheets onto the face of the bead core, being sure not to trap any air. Allow this assembly to sit for 10 minutes. Using a tissue blade, carefully trim the screen-printed veneer flush with the edges of the face of the bead core. Place the bead onto a ceramic tile with the printed veneer side up, cure, and allow it to cool completely.

3. Using a small, fine-tipped brush, apply a thin coat of gold-leaf size onto the areas of the bead core that are exposed between the "shattered" veneer, taking care not to touch any printed surfaces on the face veneer. If you do get size on a printed surface, use a damp paper towel to wipe it off immediately. Let the size dry just until it is tacky; then apply the gold leaf to the area using a gilder's brush. Brush away the excess. Let the gold leaf dry overnight. Use a soft cloth to buff the printed surfaces of the chunk bead to a light sheen. Redrill the holes with a #50 drill bit. String the chunk bead onto a necklace cable.

VISUALIZING THE LAYERS

I begin a silk-screening project by deciding if adding layer upon layer of paint color and different stencil patterns will add to the design of the piece. It is important to the success of the project to be able to visualize what the combined layers of paint will look like as you add each color and pattern. You may want to consider applying successively lighter shades of color, changing the orientation of the stencil as you progress and using a different stencil to add the final touch to the last layer. I have used a combination of all these techinques to create my final piece.

1. Apply a mix of iridescent pearl (fine), quinacridone red, quinacridone gold, and iridescent bright gold (fine) using your chosen stencil.

2. Apply a mix of iridescent bright gold (fine) and diarylide yellow, shifting the same stencil to the left or right of the first layer.

3. Apply a layer using only interference violet (fine), orienting the same stencil just slightly above the previous layer.

4. Finally, apply a mix of iridescent pearl (fine), phthalo blue (red shade), and interference violet (fine), using a stencil with a completely different pattern.

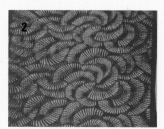
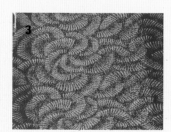
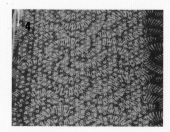

"I have found that by surrounding myself with projects that utilize [hundreds of various materials, processes, and procedures], they start to 'talk' to each other."

Swingin' Pendant

At any one time I usually have fifteen to twenty projects in progress on my workbench. This is not because I can't finish what I'm working on or because I procrastinate. Rather, it's due to the fact that over the years of working with literally hundreds of various materials, processes, and procedures, I have found that by surrounding myself with projects that utilize these in different ways, the projects I am working with start to "talk" to each other. By this, I mean that a patterned piece of polymer in a necklace may inform my choice of a hammer texture in a piece of sterling silver in a ring, which may in turn spur me to employ a broken bicycle reflector in a bracelet. I am amazed at the depth and breadth of the conversation these projects enter into. I wonder sometimes about what may happen on my bench when I'm not present.

This pendant showcases my philosophy on polymer inclusions. The polymer is neutral in both color and texture, which allows me to shift the emphasis to the "objects" selected. For this pendant I placed loose pearls under a small domed piece of plastic and meaningful words under a shard of glass. You can select your own objects, but remember that all additions to the polymer must be secured in some way, such as by tabs, a piece of glass, or even a domed piece of plastic—all three techniques are discussed below.

PREVIOUS PAGE: Robert Dancik, *Swingin' Pendant*, 2011; polymer, copper, glass, Plexiglas, and copper chain; pendant: 3¼ x 1¼ x ⅜ inches (8.5 x 3 x 0.9cm); chain: 26 inches (66cm). Photograph by Richard K. Honaman Jr.

SUPPLIES

- polymer toolbox (see page 16)
- **polymer:** 1 oz. (28g) translucent; ½ oz. (14g) black; ½ oz. (14g) gold (I used Premo! Sculpey, as it offers a terrific combination of durability, color, and predictable workability.)
- ruler
- fine-tipped permanent marker
- copper sheet, 24-gauge, minimum 5 x 3 inches (12.5 x 7.5cm)
- jeweler's saw frame
- jeweler's saw blades, 2/0
- steel bench block or similar
- ball-peen hammer
- bench pin
- beeswax
- medium-cut jeweler's files
- wet/dry sandpaper, 320-, 400-, and 600-grit

- variable-speed drill or handheld drill
- drill bits, # 30 and #52
- brass brush
- wire cutter
- copper wire, 16-gauge, 26½ inches (67.5cm)
- dull butter knife
- round-nose pliers
- patina supplies of your choice (for example, for a heat patina, which I used: filled butane torch and safety setup, including a fire brick or soldering block and bowl of cold water)
- compass or circle template
- Plexiglas
- toaster oven or craft heat gun
- dap and dapping punches
- masking tape
- small container of water

- white glue
- broken piece of glass
- words or images on paper
- burnt umber acrylic paint
- soft, damp, lint-free cloth
- short-bristle brush
- brown shoe polish
- two-part epoxy or E-6000 adhesive
- cross-peen hammer
- objects (e.g., rice pearls, beads, etc.)
- micro bolts and nuts, #0–80 (3 sets) round-face hammer

Optional
- vise
- wire-coiling tool

BOXES

1. Using a ruler and a permanent marker, measure and mark a 2¼ x 2¾-inch (5.5 x 7cm) rectangle on the copper sheet. Then measure and mark a 1¾ x 1½-inch (4.5 x 3.8cm) rectangle alongside the first. Using a jeweler's saw, cut out both rectangles.

    Using a permanent marker, draw another set of lines, ¼-inch (6mm) in from the four edges on each of the two rectangles.

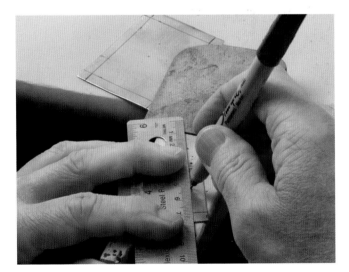

2. Place a rectangle onto the steel bench block. Using the ball-peen, strike the back of the rectangle to texture it. Repeat for the other rectangle.

3. Stabilize the large rectangle on your bench pin. Saw the line at each corner of the top edge, working only to the horizontal line. Repeat for the bottom edge. Repeat for the smaller rectangle, keeping in mind the horizontal and vertical lines.

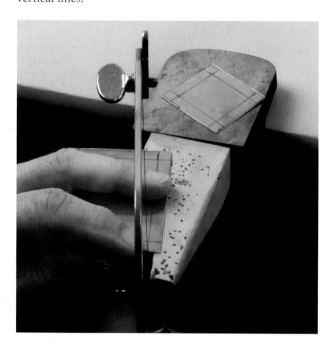

NOTE: On the larger measured rectangle, the long side will be the vertical side and the short side the horizontal side. The reverse is true for the smaller rectangle.

4. Using a drill fitted with the #52 drill bit, drill a hole in the center of each corner of each piece. Spin a #30 drill bit or jeweler's file in the drill holes to remove any metal burrs—do not enlarge the holes.

5. Place the large rectangle into the vise, stabilizing the long side in the jaws. Fold the side 90 degrees along the lines drawn in step 1. Alternately, you can use a pair of flat-nose pliers. Using jeweler's files and 400-grit sandpaper, file and sand all cut edges. Repeat for the other sides. This will yield tabs at all four corners. Fold the tabs down flat against the shorter sides.

6. Using the holes in the tabs as a guide and using the #52 drill bit, drill through the box sides. This is best done on the end of the bench pin. Scrub both boxes with a brass brush, inside and out, in preparation for the patina.

METAL CONNECTIONS

1. Using wire cutters, cut two 3-inch (7.5cm) and two 2-inch (5cm) pieces of 16-gauge wire. These will be the "staples" to secure the sides of each box together. Using flat-nose pliers, bend one 3-inch (7.5cm) length of wire ¾ inch (2cm) from one end. Insert the bent end into one of the holes in the larger box along the short side. Using the other hole on this side as a guide, make a mark on the wire where the other bend needs to be—do not bend the wire yet.

   Repeat this for the other end of the large box. Repeat for the smaller box, using the 2-inch (5cm) wire and bending it ½ inch (13mm) from the end.

2. Cut one 6-inch (15cm) and one 8-inch (20.5cm) piece of 16-gauge wire. Using a coiling tool or a pair of round-nose pliers, form each length of wire into a coil ¼ inch (6mm) in diameter. Insert a dull butter knife between each loop in the coils; then twist, opening up space. Repeat with each loop, working across both coils.

3. Insert the coil made from the 8-inch (20.5cm) wire onto the staple for the top of the large box. Bend the wire at the mark so that it is perpendicular to the bend created in step 1. (This second end will be longer than the first.) Insert the staple into the top of the box and cinch (bend) the ends of the wire on the inside of the box.

4. Place the coil made from the 6-inch (15cm) wire onto the staple for the bottom of the large box. Add the 2-inch (5cm) staple for the top of the small box. Bend both staples into place accordingly.

5. Insert the other 2-inch (5cm) staple in the bottom of the small box and cinch. With a pair of round-nose pliers, grasp the center of the bottom wire on the small box and twist one way then the other, forming a small bump for interest, or creating a spot to hang a drop. Patina the boxes and wires with a gentle heat, liver of sulfur, or other method. (I used a heat patina for this piece.)

6. Draw 3 teardrop-shaped tabs on 24-gauge copper sheet, measuring approximately ⅜ x ⅛ inch (9 x 3mm), to secure the domed plastic. Refer to Technique: Forming a Domed Piece of Plastic on page 108. In the center of the round end of each tab, drill a hole using a #52 drill bit. Using a jeweler's saw, cut out the tabs; then file and sand the edges.

POLYMER INCLUSIONS

1. Condition 1 oz. (28g) of translucent polymer. Pinch out the polymer to roughly the shape and size of the large box. Push the polymer into the box, making sure it gets into the corners. Repeat for the small box. Trim the polymer in each box, allowing it to rise just slightly above the edges.

   Using tools of your choice, make indentations at least ¹⁄₁₆-inch (1.5mm) deep into the polymer in the large box; these indents will be filled with an inlay.

2. Glue the shard of glass to the paper with words. Let the adhesive cure. Trim around the glass. Press the glass into the polymer so that you can see the outline; then remove the glass. Dig out a bit of polymer from underneath where the glass will be positioned. Reposition the glass and press the polymer against it so it sits flush.

   Cure the pendant according to manufacturer's instructions. Remove from the oven and cool.

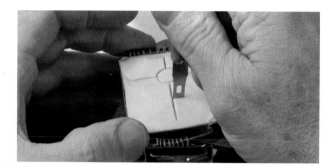

TECHNIQUE: FORMING A DOMED PIECE OF PLASTIC

1. Using a compass or circle template, scribe a circle approximately the same size as the diameter of the dome you wish to make onto the paper covering on the Plexiglas. Using the jeweler's saw, cut out the circle and remove the paper covering. It is not necessary to file the edges.

2. Place the circle in a preheated, 275° F (135° C) toaster oven for 3 to 4 minutes. Check the circle: It should start to resemble a cooked lasagna noodle—pliable but still holding its shape. Once the circle is heated, place it in the dap and put the punch on it; hold the punch in place for a minute or so. Remove the now-domed circle; it should be cool to the touch.

3. Fold a 1½-inch (3.8cm) piece of masking tape in half, allowing the ends to bend out at right angles away from the tape. This forms "wings" and essentially makes a handle. Push the wings against the top of the dome so that you can hold on to it.

4. Place a piece of 320-grit sandpaper on a smooth, even surface, and drip some water onto it. Holding the tape handle, place the dome on the wet sandpaper and rub it on the sandpaper in a figure-eight motion until the edges are sanded down. Work until the edge of the dome is sharp and even.

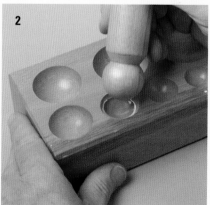

3. Condition the black and gold polymer. Roll each color to a snake with a ⅛-inch (3mm) diameter. Place the two snakes side by side and twist them together. Roll the twisted snake to a 1/16-inch (1.5mm) diameter. Use this snake as the inlay in the large box, pressing it into the recess made in step 1. Cure the box again and cool. Carefully remove the piece of glass.

4. Once cooled, sand the polymer flush to the top of the copper boxes, starting with files then progressing to 320-grit wet/dry sandpaper and working up to 600-grit. Follow by rubbing the piece with the back of the sandpaper and a lot of water, creating a nice, smooth finish.

METAL FASTENERS

1. Put the dome into position and place the teardrop-shaped tabs (created in step 6 of Metal Connections on page 107) around the perimeter of the dome. Using a fine-tipped permanent marker, mark the tab drill-hole placement into the polymer, and set the tabs aside. Using a drill fitted with a #52 drill bit, drill through the polymer and the copper box. Check the fit; adjust if necessary. Remove all the pieces and patina the tabs to match the rest of the metal.

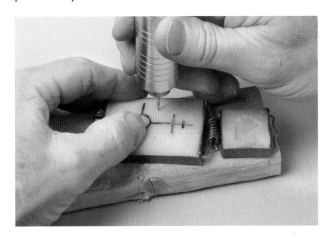

2. Using the sharp edge of a craft knife, make a few random light cuts in the surface of the polymer; this will add an additional aged look to the piece. Rub the burnt umber acrylic paint all over the surface of the piece; then, using a damp cloth, immediately rub off as much of the paint as you would like. Set aside to dry. Using a short bristle brush, apply a very little bit of brown shoe polish over the piece. Allow to dry for at least 30 minutes; then buff. **NOTE**: The paint adds color in the lines and is more distinct than shoe polish. The shoe polish in turn adds a patina and depth that you can't get any other way.

Using two-part epoxy or E-6000 adhesive, glue the shard of glass back into its place in the small box. Using a cross-peen hammer or even a dull butter knife, upset the edges of the box. This will create an uneven surface, which works well with the look of the overall design, adds interest to the piece, and creates a bit of reflection once burnished.

3. Set the objects (I used pearls), the dome, and the teardrop-shaped tabs into place. Using the micro bolts and nuts, secure the tabs to the box.

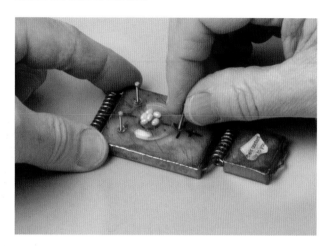

4. Using wire cutters, trim the bolts on the back side of the box, down to the nuts. Place the box face down onto a metal block, positioned so that the dome is not on the block; then gently hammer the ends of the bolts using a round-faced hammer.

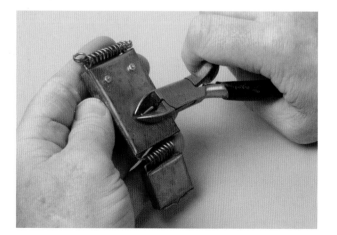

5. Cut a 2½-inch (6.5cm) piece of 16-gauge copper wire; then texture and patina it to match the piece. Roll a loop or two in one end. Insert the straight end through the coil at the top of the large box; then create a loop on the other end to secure the wire in place. The loops will be used as the hanger/bail for the pendant once complete.

Boats with Gossamer Waves

Prior to the week together, Robert and Seth communicated a number of times by phone and e-mail. They quickly determined that Robert would create a metal neckpiece that Seth would fill with polymer. They felt comfortable with the independent work they would accomplish—and that this project would highlight each of their strengths.

Robert mailed Seth several curved copper pieces that could be incorporated into the type of finished piece they had discussed. Inspired by their upcoming trip to the Outer Banks, they decided to use boat-shaped forms. However, Seth requested that the pieces be made of silver instead of copper, as he wanted the color to come from the polymer. While Robert was fond of the copper, he understood Seth's concern that it would dictate his polymer palette. He wanted Seth to have the freedom to choose his polymer technique, so he deferred to Seth's request. Because fabricating sterling silver is time-consuming, Robert arrived at the beach with a fully formed necklace and earrings.

Deciding upon Separate Workspaces

Upon arrival at the house, Robert set up his workspace surrounded by the comfort of others working in metal—Julie and Wendy. He knew they would understand and even enjoy the noise and his penchant for spreading out beyond his official space. His centralized location was definitely a plus, as he quickly became the go-to guy for a quick sawing or soldering, a particular tool or fastener. As his part of the collaboration with Seth was complete, he was a generous and happy participant in others' work.

Seth took his time choosing a place to work and settled on the marble bar top in the middle of the kitchen. Here he could keep the space to himself so he could concentrate on his work, but also join in the surrounding conversations.

TOP: After reviewing a number of Robert's copper prototypes, they decided to use boat-shaped pieces to form a necklace. Seth requested that Robert use silver, as he thought it was less ethnic, more modern, and more neutral.
ABOVE: Having completed the necklace and earrings at home, Robert was able to more fully concentrate on exploring with Seth what might fill the "boats."

TECHNIQUE: FORMING THE BOATS

1. Cut a 1 x 2¾–inch (2.5 x 7cm) piece from a sheet of 24-gauge silver. Draw a line down the center lengthwise. Set the piece in a vise so the line meets the top of the vise. Using a mallet, fold the metal 90 degrees along the line. After the metal is folded, remove it from the vise, put it onto a steel block, and hammer it the rest of the way flat. Next, draw a boat shape, with the fold used as the bottom of the boat.

2. Cut out the shape with a saw or shears. File the edges. Brush on a coating of flux, and then either hold the shape with a pair of heat-resistant tweezers or place it on a heatproof surface. Using a torch, anneal the piece by heating the metal just until it turns a dull orange color, and then immediately remove the heat source. Place the piece on a metal block to cool it. Don't quench it in water, or the water will squirt all over when you begin the forging. Line up the folded edge of the boat with the edge of the block. Tilt your head (just a little so you can observe the hammer blows, making sure they are more on the fold). As you forge with the cross-peen hammer, check the shape of the indentations the hammer makes in the metal. Each indentation should be deeper and wider at the folded edge, tapering to a point at center.

TIP: As you work, turn the boat so the edge of the metal is on the edge of the block. Strike the piece along the edge, working until the folded edge is curved and the open edge is essentially straight.

3. Using a ¹⁄₁₆-inch (1.5mm) drill bit, drill a hole ½ inch (13mm) in from each end. This hole will be used for connecting the boats together later. Anneal the piece again, and quench in water. Use a dull knife to pry the boat open.

NOTE: If needed, place the pieces in warmed pickle to remove any firescale that may have occurred from heating the silver.

4. Repeat steps 1–3, making as many boats as you would like for your necklace plus perhaps two more for a matching pair of earrings. Attach the boats together using jump rings. or create ball-tip headpins to form connectors. Add a purchased clasp or design your own, as Robert has done. (For forming your own ball-tip headpins, see instructions for Technique: Drawing a Bead on a Wire, page 129.)

Forming a Narrative

Robert, an avid storyteller, had discussed with Jeff and Seth at their first meeting the importance to him of having a narrative to describe his pieces. He typically writes these vignettes after the piece is made. Since he had completed his metalwork, he offered to write a story that might help set the mood of the collaboration. Seth was initially ambivalent about this idea but acceded to Robert's desire. Robert emerged twenty minutes later with a detailed work of fiction worthy of any good beach read—evoking the surroundings of the Outer Banks.

"Robert and Seth forged their bicoastal collaboration around a narrative—a story penned by Robert. Aided by this context, the two worked somewhat independently, consulting one another along the way. The result is a duet of perspectives and materials commingled into a harmonious whole, revealed in metal and polymer with their individual, yet distinct, styles."

—Jeff

| ROBERT'S STORY |

Janel always knew she would return to the sea. It had been thirteen years since she had left Pencault-sur-Mer and her beloved Uncle Trebor. She had missed terribly his bright smile, the perfumes of the sea air, and the feel of the warm sand beneath her feet. She remembered, with great fondness, how she would play at the water's edge beneath the imposing granite cliffs that towered above the small fishing village in the south of France. She recalled, too, how she would eat sausage, bread, and cheese with her uncle in the evening as the sun set on the watery horizon.

Now, as she was returning, she was beside herself with excitement at the prospect of seeing her uncle and telling him of her great adventures at Bodmin University in Cornwall, and of the young man with whom she had fallen in love. The cars rattled and the brakes complained every time the train had to slow for an errant animal on the tracks. She began to rub, as she had so many times before, the links of her favorite necklace—the one she wore whenever she was happy or sad; excited or lonely; and certainly on every special occasion. It was a necklace made from the tiny boats her Uncle Trebor had created and presented to her on each of her seven birthdays after her father had died and before she had gone to England to study.

Janel's mother had passed while bringing her daughter into the world, and her father had been taken by the sea just before her third birthday. Uncle Trebor had taken her in and raised her as his own. He had never married, and so he became both mother and father to his niece upon the demise of his older brother.

The first time Uncle Trebor had given Janel one of these small silver boats she thought it was an unusually cruel gesture from her normally lovely and loving uncle.

"But Uncle," she cried, "it was in a boat on the sea that my poor father died."

"I know, little one, but it was on the sea that your father was most at peace."

So, for Janel, this necklace of small boats, with their smooth tops and textured hulls, became a symbol of her father's happiness and peace of mind as well as a bittersweet reminder of the time never spent with him. *Time,* she thought, *that perhaps would have allowed me to know the spirit of the sea that my father had so dearly embraced.*

As the train squealed to a stop, she held fast one of the boat links, closed her eyes, inhaled deeply, and let the tears track gently down her cheeks.

When Seth read the story he was surprised how the misty, veiled imagery of water and waves in the story brought to mind certain elements that he wanted to carry through to the final piece.

Establishing a Palette

Taking a cue from Lindly's study of palettes, Seth chose to tint translucent polymer with hints of opaque polymer in various shades that he felt matched the melancholy notes of the story. Robert, who doesn't believe he is adept at using color, was surprised by the texture and translucency of the polymer palette that Seth had selected. He remarked that the choice completely changed what he thought the piece might look like. Seth agreed; the story and churning of the sea from the storms outside had informed his choice of color, a complete turnaround from what he had initially planned.

Thinking he would fill each silver boat with "waves" of translucent color, Seth tested several ideas for creating the waves. First, he created gill-shaped pieces in varying saturations and thicknesses to see how it would translate being housed in the boat. This process allowed him to evaluate the color change against the depth of the boat and color of the silver.

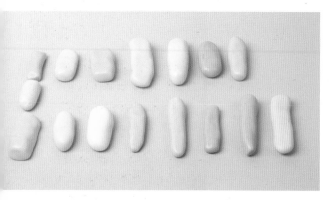

ABOVE: As the ocean changed through the phases a nor'easter imposes, so did the colors Seth created as samples for use in the boats.

RIGHT: Originally Seth throught he would fill the boat-shaped silver pieces with textured opaque colors, but reading Robert's story brought to mind the sea and gossamer waves.

"I was surprised at how well working from a narrative helped me move my work forward, and I will be taking that away with me. The project also helped me come up with a new technique for creating the gill forms and surface."

—*Seth*

Navigating Process

After consulting with Robert, Seth settled on a blue and green palette. Seth originally had hoped to fill each boat with thin, precured "gills" to create the waves, but he found it tedious and a bit problematic. Silver, being nonporous, presented a method that would dictate their process. Robert suggested that, because the top edges of the boat were upset, the polymer would have an edge to adhere to. Seth used a stiff blade to slice hundreds of waves into each boat of polymer. The pieces were cured and then resliced with a tissue blade while they were still warm to separate the waves, as some tended to fuse together.

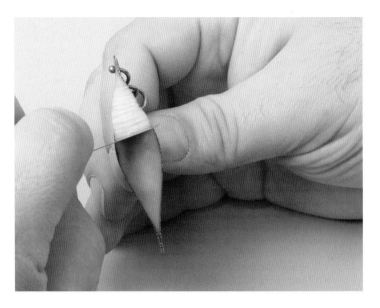

ABOVE: As is his nature, Seth did test pieces to ensure that the "waves" would stay securely in the boats and that reslicing would sometimes be necessary.

LEFT: Seth and Robert consulted on just the perfect palette of blues and greens to mesh with the theme of Robert's watery story. Viewing the baked results of Seth's tests helped Robert see how the translucent polymer would translate. When Seth read the story he was surprised how the misty, veiled imagery of water and waves in the story brought to mind certain elements that he wanted to carry through to the final piece.

"I will now play with the translucency of the polymer and adding color. I see this as a broadening of my base and the possibilities that can occur."

—*Robert*

MIX IT UP
Julie Picarello, Wendy Wallin Malinow, and Judy Belcher

At first glance, Julie, Wendy, and Judy undoubtedly present as unlikely collaborators. Julie has a calm and muted palette that plays beautifully off the metal she incorporates in her jewelry. She sketches out her ideas roughly but won't commit a design to polymer until she can almost completely envision it. Wendy creates finely detailed sketches that she eventually transfers into mixed-media jewelry and sculpture that is visually lush in high-energy colors. Judy brings her vibrant and active jewelry designs to life in polymer rather than on paper, working hands-on through each phase.

Would this union prove to be a recipe for collaborative disaster? Hardly! Differing design approaches aside, this team was closely aligned in temperament, personality, and background—perhaps more so than any other. The years each had spent navigating the corporate jungle gave them skills akin to gardening. One person planted a seed of an idea; the others watered it until it sprouted and flowered—or, if discovered to be a weed, gently *but firmly* uprooted it. Their common approach to collaborating gave them absolute freedom to mix it up— aesthetically and in terms of process. The end result was described best by Wendy as a "cabinet of curiosities." Watching each piece move and acknowledging the wonder it produces in viewers' eyes, the team agreed this collaboration was worth each late night.

OPPOSITE/COLLABORATIVE PROJECT: Julie Picarello, Wendy Wallin Malinow, and Judy Belcher, *Cabinet of Curiosities!*, 2011; polymer, wood box, various ephemera and hardware, acrylic paint, and colored pencil; 27 x 16 x 4 inches (68.5 x 40.5 x 10cm). Photograph by Richard K. Honaman Jr.

My career as an integrated circuit designer appeals greatly to my logical and analytical nature, yet there are times that—even for me—it is too intensely left-brained. To compensate over the years, I have balanced my engineering world with forays into artistic pursuits such as glassblowing, lampworking, silversmithing, metal etching, bookmaking, enameling, and more.

It wasn't until 2004 and my introduction to polymer that I became truly passionate about an art medium. My love of color, symmetry, and clean lines as well as the joy of mixing media are all reflected in my work. Inspired by the *mokume gane* technique of Tory Hughes, I began experimenting with various tools and methods of creating controlled, rather than random, patterns, and adding depth and dimension to my polymer designs. In 2006 I also began repurposing metal objects such as washers, vintage watch parts, and miniature car and railroad parts into my jewelry. I believe that transitioning a functional object into a decorative element adds a sense of whimsy to a design. It becomes art with attitude and plays a joyful tune of its own.

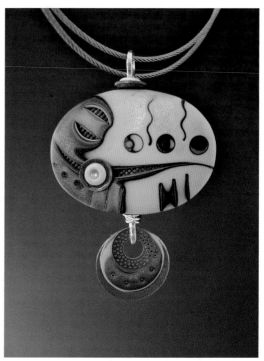

LEFT: *Button Blossoms*, 2011; polymer, sterling silver, copper, and bronze wire, vintage buttons, textured metal with patina, wire mesh, and filigree; dimensions variable. Photograph by Julie Picarello. Rather than utilizing a wire rivet, these blossoms are joined with a "polymer rivet" that anchors them together.

ABOVE: *Ada*, 2009; polymer, steel cable, hammered sterling, copper, bone, and metallic pulver; 2 x 1½ inches (5 x 3.8cm). Photograph by Julie Picarello. Using ivory as negative background space brings the design forward and gives it more impact.

Jordan's Hope, 2011; polymer, sterling silver, hammered steel, plaster washer, ceramic bead, and hand-dyed silk; 2½ x 1½ inches (6.5 x 3.8cm). Photograph by Julie Picarello. The polymer in this work was inspired by and custom-mixed to match the hand-dyed silk. This piece was created to raise funds for a young woman's trip to the Mayo Clinic.

SHOWCASE WENDY WALLIN MALINOW

I grew up on the Oregon coast, and nature is a big part of who I am and what I create. Growing up in a family of artists, obtaining a fine arts education in drawing and painting, and then having a career as an illustrator and art director led to a somewhat fragmented path of artistic pursuit. I started working with polymer in the late 1980s when I saw Pier Voulkos's work in an exhibit in Portland, Oregon. Polymer, as a medium, allowed me to continue my sculpting in a smaller format as well as integrate favorite materials and imagery. I was hooked!

For conceptual inspiration, *The Artist's Way* author Julia Cameron suggests continually filling your "well"—a stockpile of internalized images and ideas to draw from in your art. Some of the things that inspire me are children's art, nature, friends' spirits and their stories, other respected artists' creative pursuits, melody and lyrics, winter wonderlands, anything that sparkles or shines (frost, water, dew, and so forth), Dr. Seuss, *The Wizard of Oz*, the zoo, trolls, human anatomy and physics, weird science, chaos theory, glitter, spangles, and always, *always*, candy. These all help to stock the visual stew that slowly swirls around in my head.

LEFT: *Row, Row, Row Your Log*, 2011; polymer; 4 x 2 x ½ x 11 inches (10.2 x 6.4 x 28cm). Photograph by Courtney Frisse. The log canoe is actually a box whose watery lid of polymer "rowers" opens to reveal a spring-green "meadow" with flowers, sky, daisies, and a robin's egg hidden inside.

ABOVE: *My Happy Place*, 2011; polymer and glitter; 5½ x 5½ inches (14 x 14cm). Photograph by Courtney Frisse. The outside of this cuff is a lush, surreal landscape, with a pastel snail, Life Saver candy, mushroom, striped grass, and so forth; the inside is hollow and filled with dirt, skulls, worms, and roots—the underbelly of nature or happiness.

Sugar Links, 2011; polymer and glitter; 1¾ x 28 inches (4.5 x 71cm). Photograph by Courtney Frisse. This chain necklace features hand-sculpted links of textured and embellished polymer. I added a patina of glass glitter for a subtle sheen.

My parents nurtured a childhood filled with creative endeavors—after-school art classes, trips to museums, and summers filled with travel. As I grew older, my sensible choice of a degree in finance was equally satisfying to me, but I filled my evenings in the studio with friends from the fine arts department. I balanced twenty years as an accountant with evening workshops learning about ceramics (the wheel was not kind to me, but I loved the slab roller and extruder) and watercolor painting (where I formed an appreciation of blending colors).

I love that I have found a way of incorporating equally the left and right sides of my brain to sculpt a career in polymer. My meticulously crafted jewelry is filled with bright and joyful colors, celebrating techniques and designs that employ logic and spontaneity. Similarly, I have balanced that solitary work by surrounding myself with people. I truly enjoy coordinating conferences and teaching workshops, and I enjoyed organizing everyone for this book. Rather than squelching the constant struggle that must go on inside my head, I embrace it and claim the mantle of "creatively organized."

LEFT: *Twirl in Red*, 2008; polymer and sterling silver; pendant: 1½ x 1⅛ inches (3.8 x 2.9cm); chain: 18 inches (45.5cm). Photograph by Greg Staley. This piece is from a kinetic line of jewelry featuring central beads that twirl independently of the pendant to reveal different canework.

ABOVE: *Fancy Stones*, 2011; polymer; dimensions variable. Photograph by Judy Belcher. These "stones," which range in diameter from 3 to 5 inches [7.5 to 12.5cm] and are made to hang flat, flowing down a wall, were inspired by Cynthia's use of polymer in her home.

Polymer Knitting, 2011, polymer and gunmetal chain, 24 x 4 (at the widest) inches (61 x 10cm).
Photograph by Judy Belcher. "I am not a knitter, but I love Missoni knits and wanted to replicate the look
and feel in polymer. I'm thrilled with how this necklace does just that," says Belcher.

"If you imagine metal and polymer mediums as music, then metal is a marching band, full of force and vigor. . . . Polymer is like an ever-changing radio dial, with the ability to morph from primitive drums to elegant arias to bluesy jazz without missing a beat."

Imprint *Mokume* Totem Necklace

To me, there is a perfect, almost indescribable, sense of rightness when working with metal and polymer. If you imagine metal and polymer mediums as music, then metal is a marching band, full of force and vigor. It tempts the listener to use sharp tools and hot torches, to abandon restraint and hammer with glee. Polymer is like an ever-changing radio dial, with the ability to morph from primitive drums to elegant arias to bluesy jazz without missing a beat. Play them together, and they hum with endless possibilities of color, texture, and form.

This project incorporates sticks of patterned polymer, hammered and textured metal tubing, and a variety of repurposed and riveted metal pieces to form an asymmetrical totem pendant. Collect and choose items from hardware stores, hobby shops, and vintage stores—anywhere your eye leads you and whatever works with your design.

OPPOSITE: Julie Picarello, *Imprint Mokume Totem Necklace*; polymer, hammered copper tubing, punched silver disks, copper mesh, disk break, copper wire, vintage copper chain, and hand-forged copper clasp; pendant: 2 x 2½ inches (5 x 6.5cm); chain: 18 inches (45.5cm). Photograph by Richard K. Honaman Jr.

SUPPLIES

- polymer toolbox (see page 16)
- **polymer:** 2 oz. (57g) turquoise; 1 oz. (28g) gold; 1 oz. (28g) ecru; 1 oz. (28g) pearl; 1 oz. (28g) peacock pearl; 1 oz. (28g) 18K gold; 1 oz. (28g) cadmium red (I used Premo! Sculpey, as it imparts a smooth fusion between layers when it is sliced.)
- measuring tool
- smooth ceramic tile
- spray bottle filled with water
- tools of your choice for imprinting (cutters with clean edges, brass tubing, carving tools, hardware, and so forth)
- nonslip pad
- deli paper (4)
- texturing material (i.e., linen fabric, scrubbing sponge)
- wet/dry sandpaper, 400-, 600-, 800-, and 1000-grit
- soft cloth
- round copper tubing, ¹⁄₃₂-inch (0.8mm) diameter, 4 inches (10cm)
- steel bench block
- ball-peen hammer
- riveting hammer
- metal shears
- jeweler's file
- round-nose pliers
- half-hard copper wire, 20-gauge, 6 inches (15cm)
- liquid polymer
- ball stylus
- dust mask
- metal pulver
- metal accent pieces (see image on page 128 for some of my favorites)
- variable-speed drill
- drill bits, #50 and #65
- permanent marker
- ball-tip headpin, 20-gauge (if you aren't making one; see Technique: Drawing a Bead on a Wire, page 129)
- nail set
- table vise
- chain or necklace

Optional (for making a ball-tip headpin)
- butane torch
- butane fuel
- flush cutters
- sterling silver round wire, 20-gauge
- insulated tweezers with fiber grip
- fiber block or heatproof tile
- bowl filled with cold water
- soap
- polishing cloth

IMPRINT MOKUME STICKS

1. To replicate the four soft and muted colors shown below, combine turquoise, gold, and ecru (for color #1); ecru and pearl (for color #2); peacock pearl and ecru (for color #3); and cadmium red, 18K gold, and ecru (for color #4). Roll each of your four colors through the thickest setting of the pasta machine, and then cut them into 2 x 3–inch (5 x 7.5cm) rectangles. Stack a darker and lighter shade rectangle together and roll them through the pasta machine on the thickest setting. Repeat with the other two rectangles. Maintaining the dark and light ordering, stack the resulting 2 sheets and roll through the pasta machine one last time. This will result in a single, very long, four-color strip. Cut it into 4 equal sections and stack them, still maintaining the same ordering.

2. Using an acrylic brayer, firmly roll the stack until it is securely adhered to a smooth ceramic tile. Trim the edges so they are uniform and even. Lightly spritz the stack with water. The water will work as a release and keep your tools from sticking to the polymer. Impress a variety of tools into the stack of polymer. Keep your finished design in mind as you work. Be sure to keep your impressions in a row so each row can complete a "stick" when they are cut in step 4.

3. Place the ceramic tile onto a nonslip pad. Carefully grip the ends of the tissue blade with two hands, between the thumb and index fingers. Set your hands on the work surface on either side of the stack, with the edges of your little fingers touching the work surface. The key is not how thin or thick the slice is, but rather that you maintain a consistent thickness throughout the slice. Set the blade into the back edge of the polymer, approximately $^1/_{16}$ inch (1.5mm) from the top of the stack, and pull the blade toward you through the polymer. As you remove slices from the stack, set them aside on a piece of deli paper. Typically, each stack will yield 4 to 8 slices, depending on the thickness desired.

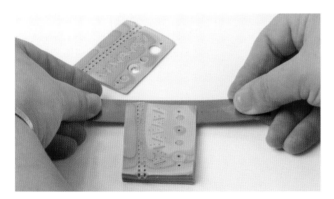

TIP: To facilitate consistency, focus on your hands rather than your blade as you slice. If your hands are set firmly on the work surface as you draw them toward you, the blade will follow along and maintain an even depth throughout the slice.

4. For strength, the sticks need to be at least $^1/_8$ inch (3mm) thick. To add thickness to your slices, roll out a sheet of turquoise polymer on the thickest setting. Texture one side of the polymer sheet (optional) and place it texture side down onto a piece of deli paper. Set the imprinted slice of polymer (from step 3) onto the polymer sheet, lay a piece of deli paper over the slice, and use your fingers or an acrylic brayer to gently smooth the two layers together.

Cut the imprinted slices into 3 sticks, each approximately 1½ inches (3.8cm) long. When cutting, carefully bend the tissue blade into a shallow curve and cut slightly inward to bevel the top edge of the polymer stack.

5. Place a piece of deli paper over the cut piece and use it to help smooth the beveled edges down, creating a clean and slightly rounded edge. Cure the sticks according to manufacturer's instructions. Using 400-, 600-, 800-, and 1000-grit wet/dry sandpaper in progression, sand the sticks, and then gently buff with a soft cloth for a gentle sheen.

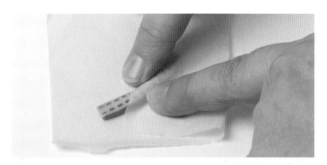

TUBULAR TOTEMS

1. To create the supporting spine for the sticks, place the copper tubing on a steel bench block, and using the flat edge of a ball-peen hammer, slowly hammer up and down the length of the tubing until it is almost completely flat. Use the narrow edge of a riveting hammer to add lines of texture to the metal.

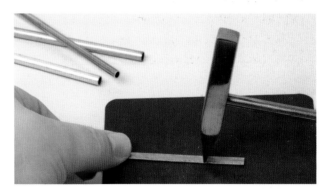

2. Using metal shears, trim one end of the spine, and then smooth it with a jeweler's file. Use round-nose pliers on that end to form a loop for the hanger/bail.

3. Wrap a length of 20-gauge copper wire around the support below the bail. Cut with metal shears and file the ends of the wire smooth.

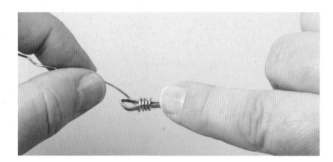

4. Place the cured sticks, imprint side down, onto a sheet of copy paper; then rest the support, centered, on top of the sticks. Roll a new sheet of turquoise polymer on a medium setting, and texture, if desired. Cut 3 strips slightly smaller than the height of each stick and just long enough to cover the width of the support, with ¼ inch (6mm) extra on each side. Dab a bit of liquid polymer onto each stick, just outside the metal spine; then gently set the strip of polymer over the support. Tap down to secure the two polymer layers together.

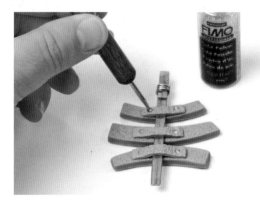

Where the polymer strip was connected with liquid polymer, press down with a ball stylus to form a rounded indentation. Put on a dust mask. Dip the ball stylus into the metal pulver, tap off the excess, and press the stylus into the indentation. This will create the look of a metal rivet while ensuring a solid connection between cured and uncured polymer. Carefully transfer the paper with the sticks and support in place onto a tile or baking tray, cure a second time, and allow to cool. Using 20-gauge wire, wrap again below the sticks to keep them from sliding off the support.

5. Now here comes the difficult part—deciding which combination of metal accent pieces to use! Some of my favorites include a disk brake set from a miniature railroad, vintage chain pieces, pipe screen mesh, and corrugated metal. For this necklace I chose a small punched-silver disk, copper wire mesh, and a disk brake.

6. Once you have selected your pieces, use a variable-speed drill fitted with a #50 drill bit to drill center holes in each piece, as needed. Stack the pieces on the spine below the sticks to finalize placement. Use a permanent marker to indicate the drill point(s) on the spine. Drill the hole(s) in the spine using a variable-speed drill fitted with a #65 drill bit. Use metal shears to trim the spine so that it ends just below the rivet point, and file smooth.

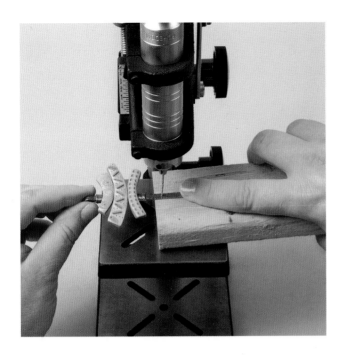

Clamp a nail set into a table vise. Place the assembled pieces, face down, so the ball-tip of the headpin rests in the nail set. Trim the headpin so about ⅛ inch (3mm) of wire remains above the support. Angle a ball-peen hammer and gently tap the wire in a circular motion. This will splay the metal out from the center so it flattens and becomes wider than the drill hole.

String the pendant on a chain or a necklace of your choice.

7. To create a fancy rivet, follow the instructions Technique: Drawing a Bead on a Wire, below, to create a ball-tip headpin; otherwise you can use a purchased headpin. Insert the headpin through the decorative pieces and the metal support.

TECHNIQUE: DRAWING A BEAD ON A WIRE

1. Following manufacturer's instructions, fill the butane torch with butane fuel.

2. Using flush cutters, cut a 1- to 1½-inch (2.5 to 3.8cm) length of 20-gauge silver wire.

3. Place one end of the wire in the tip of the insulated tweezer. The tweezer should be held horizontal, and the wire should be held vertical.

4. While holding the tweezer in your nondominant hand, position the wire over the heat-resistant tile (with the bowl of water close by). Release the safety lock on the filled butane torch and press the igniter button. Heat the base of the wire with the flame until the wire forms a ball.

5. When the ball forms, turn off the torch, let the red glow fade on the wire, and then quench the wire in cool water.

6. To remove oxides that may form on the sterling silver, wash the piece in soapy water, rinse, dry, and polish with a polishing cloth.

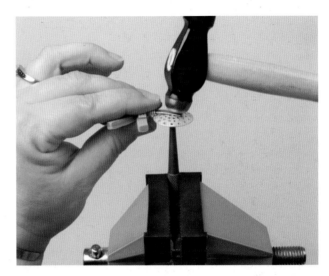

"In terms of my own work process, I receive the most pleasure and delight from thinking 'outside the lightbulb' (or 'outside the box,' whatever the phrase), just to somehow make my work different— to subvert an existing visual or idea."

Subverted Bracelet

Sometimes I find my worktable filled with many undefined blobs of polymer sprawled about and a gaping, empty workspace directly in front of me. Where do I go now? The ever-changing and sometimes elusive goal for me is to progress, grow, and basically try to please my eyes and delight my brain—and, with luck, please other viewers as well.

In terms of my own work process, I receive the most pleasure and delight from thinking "outside the lightbulb" (or "outside the box," whatever the phrase), just to somehow make my work different—to subvert an existing visual or idea. To me, subverting means working out of, and going beyond, your comfort zone. In practical terms, this can mean transforming the material in a new way, doing the opposite of what you're comfortable with, finding a different angle, a fresh style, something unexpected, a different execution.

Nothing is weirder than nature in all of its glory, especially aquatic forms, which is why I'm sharing this particular project. There is no end to the variation of shape and color. Plus, unlike, say, sculpting a human head, there is no "correct" shape to hold you back. The subject matter frees up the artist to go out of his or her particular comfort zone. The discussion should begin with what you, the individual, want to tweak visually. What do you want to evoke within your own artistic path and/or your viewer's reaction?

OPPOSITE: Wendy Wallin Malinow, *Subverted Bracelet*, 2011; polymer, powders, and resin; dimensions variable. Photograph by Richard K. Honaman Jr.

- polymer toolbox (see page 16)
- **polymer:** 2 oz. (57g) pearl; 2 oz. (57g) translucent; 1 oz. (28g) turquoise; 1 oz. (28g) purple; 1 oz. (28g) wasabi; 1 oz. (28g) cadmium red; 1 oz. (28g) orange; 1 oz. (28g) alizarin crimson; 1 oz. (28g) white; plus an occasional pinch of beige (I used Premo! Sculpey, as I like that it is malleable right out of the package.)
- Pearl Ex powders, interference and iridescent
- small paintbrush
- cone-shaped rubber tool or knitting needle, US #5 (3.75mm)
- polyester fiberfill
- needle tool
- aluminum foil
- flat-nose pliers
- small disposable craft paintbrush
- white glue
- texturing tools (i.e., scrubbing sponge, metal scouring pad, etc.)
- variable-speed or hand drill
- drill bit, #70
- clear resin (I prefers ICE Resin, as it cures clear and is self-leveling) fabric-covered elastic cord
- watchmaker's glue

TENTACLE BEADS

1. On the thickest setting of the pasta machine, condition, mix, and roll 2 pearlized sheets of polymer—first, turquoise and pearl, then purple and pearl (each in a ratio of 1:1.5). Trim each sheet to a 1 x ¾–inch (2.5 x 2cm) rectangle. Butt the short end of the sheets next to each other; then fold and roll on the thickest setting of the pasta machine, slightly blending where the two colors meet.

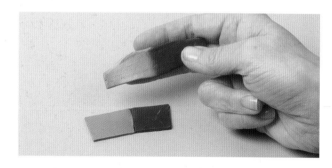

2. Working from a long end, roll up the resulting blended sheet into a snake, matching colors as you go. Smooth and blend the seam. Continue rolling, pushing each end toward the center, forming tapered ends with a thicker middle and keeping the roll to approximately 2 inches (5cm) long. One tapered end should be shorter and thicker than the other. Form the thicker taper into a spiral; twist and slightly spiral the other end.

3. Condition and roll translucent polymer into a ⅛-inch- (3mm-) diameter snake. Roll cadmium red polymer on a thin setting of the pasta machine and trim to match the length of the snake. Place the snake on the sheet of polymer, and then gently roll this assembly forward, past where the seam of the outline color should be. Roll the polymer backward, which will create a line of demarcation where the sheet of polymer overlaps itself; trim the polymer at this mark. Join the 2 edges of the outline sheet in a butted seam and roll gently to smooth the polymer so no seam is evident.

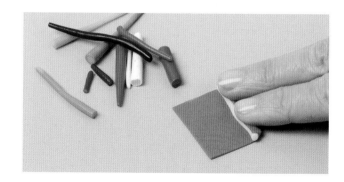

: When creating the suckers, you can either make a variety of colors or use just one that complements the tentacle, as I did with the wasabi green in step 4.

4. Roll and taper one end of the resulting bull's-eye cane to form suckers in graduated sizes. Cut 1/16-inch- (1.5mm-) thick slices, and apply them to the length of each tentacle, placing the larger suckers at the thicker end of the tentacle and the smaller suckers as you work down the length of the tentacle. Brush the suckers with Pearl Ex powders. Set beads aside.

CORAL BEADS

1. Condition cadmium red polymer and roll it into a 1-inch- (2.5cm-) diameter sphere. Make sure the sphere is completely smooth and there are no seams. Pinch out 3 extensions, forming a triad shape. Roll each point of the triad between your fingers, forming a simple 3/8-inch- (9mm-) diameter extension. Or create a simple cylinder.

2. Using a cone-shaped tool or knitting needle, indent the end of each extension approximately 1/4 inch (6mm) to resemble a hollow tube shape. Place the beads onto polyester fiberfill and cure according to manufacturer's instructions. Allow the beads to cool.

3. Condition and mix a pea-size amount of orange polymer with a walnut-size amount of cream-colored polymer (made by mixing white with a pinch of beige). For this step I prefer to use Sculpey III, as it smears well. You can mix different ratios according to your own color preferences. Roll the polymer into a 1/16 x 1-inch (1.5mm x 2.5cm) snake. Wrap the snake around the end of a tube and smear it down the side a bit so it blends into the bead. Texture the raw polymer by dragging and dotting with a needle tool. Apply a small amount of interference powder with a small brush.

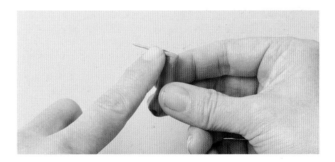

4. Condition and mix 3 parts pearl with 1 part turquoise polymer. Roll into a thin snake. Cut the snake into 1/8-inch- (3mm-) long sections, and roll the sections into small tubes and spike shapes. Using a needle tool, insert them into the ends of the tube forms or perhaps leave some tubes open. Set beads aside.

STAR BEADS

1. Condition and mix 1 part wasabi (green) with 10 parts pearl polymer. Roll this into a sphere approximately 1 inch (2.5cm) in diameter. Make sure there are no seams and that the sphere is completely smooth. Pinch out 5 extensions, forming a 5-pointed star shape. Elongate each extension by rolling and pulling each point between your fingers. Continue to smooth as you shape. Shape each pointed end into a slight curve.

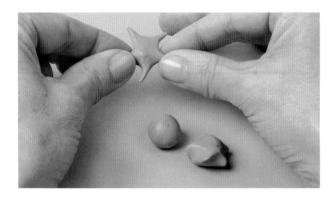

2. Using a cone-shaped tool or fat knitting needle, form a deep indention in the middle of the star. For texture and added interest, roll small balls and spikes of alizarin crimson polymer and place in the middle of the depression. Add a dot of light orange (created for the coral beads) to the center of the cluster of balls and spikes, and add a hole in the middle of the dot with a needle tool. Set beads aside.

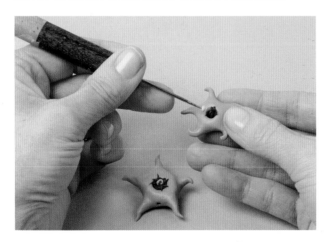

TIDE POOL BEADS

1. Condition and mix a walnut-size piece of cream-colored polymer (as described in step 3 of Coral Beads on page 133) with a pea-size amount of orange polymer. Roll the polymer on a medium-thick setting of your pasta machine.

Form a 1-inch- (2.5cm-) diameter aluminum foil ball, and then roll to compress, shaping into an organic sphere, with a few bumps and crannies. Wrap the polymer sheet around the foil ball, trimming and smoothing seams as you go.

2. Using variously sized pointed tools—a needle tool, knitting needle, even a small straw—pierce holes in the polymer, working all the way down to the foil to create texture and "windows." Carve out a bigger opening so you can fill the interior later with detail. Cure according to manufacturer's instructions and allow the bead to cool.

3. Insert an X-Acto knife into the middle of the foil ball and twist, cutting the foil up a bit. Using a needle tool, pick out the foil pieces. Use flat-nose pliers to twist and pull out hard-to-reach foil bits. This process can be a bit painstaking, but be patient—it eventually comes out and reveals an interesting hollow bead.

4. Condition alizarin crimson and roll into a thin sheet. Using a craft paintbrush, paint a thin layer of white glue along the inside of the cavity of the bead—this will offer grip for the new layer of polymer. Inlay and smooth the alizarin sheet to line the interior cavity of the bead completely.

5. Add spikes and balls to the layer of crimson for added elements inside the bead. Brush on Pearl Ex iridescent powder to highlight the interior details. Set beads aside.

SUBVERTED BRACELET

1. Gather the various beads, and place them on a piece of fiberfill. Cure according to the manufacturer's instructions and allow to cool. Using a drill and #70 drill bit, drill each bead in an appropriate place, keeping in mind how you would like the bead to hang on the bracelet.

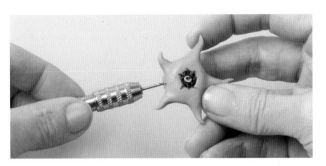

2. Finish each bead as you would like. Consider sanding, or sanding and then buffing, adding resin to some beads for a slimy effect. String each bead onto elastic cording. Tie the ends together using a surgeon's knot; then add a dab of watchmaker's glue to secure the bracelet. Alternatively, choose one shape, play with it, and repeat these beads for a chunky bracelet.

Wendy made tentacles using various Skinner Blend combinations, applied resin to the finished pieces for that "slimy" effect, and then strung them all together to create this bracelet of vibrant tentacles. Photograph by Richard K. Honaman Jr.

PLAYING WITH SHAPES AND COLOR

Aquatic, marine, and coral reef ecosystems are rich worlds with color upon color, and texture encrusted upon texture. Branch out and use your own special skills, such as complex canes, or try some new colors mixed into your favorite palettes; then apply them to the shapes you have learned or some of the following sculpted shapes.

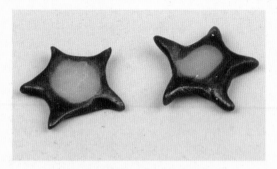

Iridescent Sea Stars

Add the appearance of a jellylike center by making a Skinner Blend jelly roll about ¾ inch (2cm) in diameter, with purple on the outside and translucent in the center polymer. (For instructions, refer to step 2 in Folded Beads on page 60.) Cut ³⁄₁₆-inch- (5mm-) thick slices. Pinch out the sides to 4 or 5 points. Add various iridescent and interference Pearl Ex powders. My favorite colors include interference blue, interference red, interference green, and duo red blue. Set beads aside.

Nudibranch

Make a Skinner Blend of purple polymer and green polymer, and roll into ⅜-inch- (9mm-) diameter snake. Pinch out 2 points on one end and taper the other end. Add texture all over the shape. Roll out tiny balls of red polymer in 3 different sizes, and then adhere each ball. Add various iridescent and interference Pearl Ex powders. Set beads aside.

Sea Squirts

Draw from your knowledge of other aquatic animals. Mix 1 part turquoise polymer to 8 parts pearl polymer, and form into a grape shape, approximately 1-inch (2.5cm) in diameter. Roll out three ³⁄₁₆-inch- (5mm-) diameter snakes of the same color. Insert thin wires into each tentacle for added strength; then attach the tentacles onto the main body. Texture and make shallow depressions. Add iridescent powder, and cure. Smear purple polymer to the ends of the tentacles. Add translucent polymer to a few of the depressions. Add more iridescent powder to the newly added, raw polymer. Set beads aside.

Double-Barreled Barnacle

Condition and form a walnut-size sphere of turquoise polymer, and roll it into a ¼-inch- (6mm-) diameter snake, tapered slightly in the middle. Texture the shape with pin tools so that it looks like wood. Roll ⅛-inch- (3mm-) diameter snakes of purple, add them to each end of the textured turquoise, and indent the ends to form the snakes into tubes. Cure. Roll out a ¹⁄₁₆-inch (1.5mm) snake of wasabi (green) polymer and smear around each end. Set beads aside.

"Much of the jewelry I create celebrates both left-brain and right-brain ways of approaching the creative process—it is visually planned and structured, yet playful and tactile."

Twirling Necklace

Much of the jewelry I create celebrates both left-brain and right-brain ways of approaching the creative process. This twirling necklace perfectly symbolizes these two tendencies—it is visually planned and structured, yet playful and tactile (quite literally, as you can spin it while you are wearing it).

If you rely more on left-brained thinking, you might enjoy making lists and drawings to plan out this necklace on paper. Consider in what order the beads will lie, keeping in mind color, pattern, size, and shape; remember that each "framing bead" and each interior "twirling center bead" can spin independently. Or you can draw on your right brain, dive in, and just make those decisions spontaneously while you are forming each bead.

Similar left-brain/right-brain strategies can be employed when making the tessellated beads. Use the left side of your brain to cut, mirror, and list the various ways your original cane can be recombined. Or exercise the right side by smashing and morphing the original cane into a new triangle and create dozens more tessellations.

PREVIOUS PAGE: Judy Belcher, *Twirling Necklace*, 2010; polymer and glass beads; 1½ x 28 inches (3.8 x 71cm). Photograph by Richard K. Honaman Jr.

SUPPLIES

- polymer toolbox (see page 16)
- **polymer:** 8 oz. (226g) scrap; 6 oz. (170g) white; 6 oz. (170g) black; 6 oz. (170g) turquoise; 6 oz. (1a70g) yellow (I used Kato Polyclay, as it holds even minute details clearly during the caning process and firms up quickly so I can immediately slice the cane.)
- round and square Kemper plunger-style cutters (graduated size sets)
- wet/dry sandpaper, 220-grit
- copy paper
- pen or pencil
- painter's tape

- variable-speed or hand drill
- drill bit, #70
- paintbrush
- repel gel
- headpin, 21-gauge (16)
- copy paper
- uncoated deli paper
- liquid polymer
- texturing material (I used Clay Yo Texture Sponges)
- round, square, and oval Ateco nesting cutters
- cornstarch
- soft medium paintbrush

- wire cutters
- flexible beading wire, .014 49-strand clasp
- black O-rings, 5mm (at least 20)
- purchased or hand-made clasp (see page 144)
- crimp beads (2)
- glass seed beads (2)
- crimping pliers

Optional
- craft stick or dowel
- double-sided tape

STRIPED AND CHECKERBOARD CANES

1. Condition and roll the black polymer on the thickest setting of the pasta machine. Repeat, conditioning and sheeting the white polymer. To create a simple striped cane, cut a 2 x 4–inch (5 x 10cm) sheet of each color and stack on top of each other. Roll across the surface with an acrylic rod to eliminate any air pockets that may be trapped between the layers. Cut this stack in half; then stack one-half on top of the other, making sure the colors alternate. Repeat so the cane has 8 layers in total.

   TIP: If you are going to cut this stack in even slices, don't stack too many layers, as it makes it more difficult to cut the slices evenly.

2. Repeat step 1 to create at least 4 other striped canes, adjusting the thickness of each stripe to alter the finished look of each cane. Using thicker (or more) sheets of either color will cause the cane to read darker or lighter.

3. Create a simple checkerboard cane by starting with an evenly striped cane made in step 1. Using a stiff blade, slice straight down from the top to the bottom of the cane, working across the stripes and creating a slice that is as wide as the thickness of each stripe.

Sit or stand so that you are looking directly down onto the cane. This will ensure that, as you slice, your blade remains exactly perpendicular to the work surface. If you are cutting straight, the blade will almost disappear.

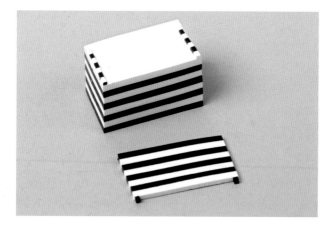

TIP: Cut a thin slice of the cane; then cut 2 small strips from the slice to be used as guides. Place the guides on top of the cane so they go down the length of each side. Use the distance between each layer as a guide for how thick to cut each slice from the cane.

4. Reassemble the slices, flipping every other one so the rows of black and white alternate from slice to slice. Gradually ease the slices together, working from back to front and making sure each line in the cane matches (black to white and white to black).

VARIOUS JELLY ROLLS

1. Roll a sheet of black polymer on the thickest setting of the pasta machine. Repeat to create a thick sheet of white. Cut a 2 x 2–inch (5 x 5cm) sheet of each color and stack them together. Roll the stack through the pasta machine two times, reducing the setting of the pasta machine with each pass, resulting in a 2 x 4–inch (5 x 10cm) sheet. With the black polymer against your work surface, angle a stiff

blade and trim each short side of the sheet to create a bevel cut. Fashion a 1/32-inch- (0.8mm-) diameter snake of white polymer. Place the snake at the edge of the sheet, and then roll up the sheet into a spiral jelly roll.

TIP: To create a variation of this spiral jelly roll, flip the sheets over so the white polymer is against the work surface and use a black snake of clay.

2. Mix 6 oz. (170g) of yellow polymer with 1/2 oz. (14g) of turquoise polymer to create the lime green color. (This will make enough of that color for the rest of the project.) Create 2 Skinner Blend jelly rolls: 1 in lime green and 1 in turquoise, by following steps 1 and 2 of Folded Beads on page 60.

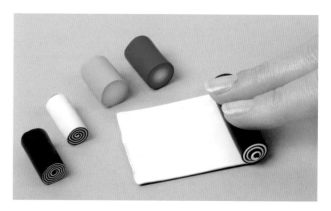

TESSELLATED MASTER CANE

1. Following the Two-Color Skinner Blend instructions on page 18, create various hues of lime green polymer and, with the pasta machine, roll each color to a 1 x 3–inch (2.5 x 7.5cm) strip on a medium thickness. Stack each strip, beginning with white and gradually getting darker, ending with the original color, to create a gradated cane. Repeat to create a gradated cane in turquoise.

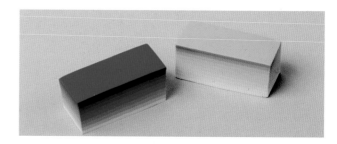

2. Turn 1 gradated cane on its side and cut 3 triangular-shaped wedges. Reserve some of each cane to use in the framing beads. Repeat for the other color.

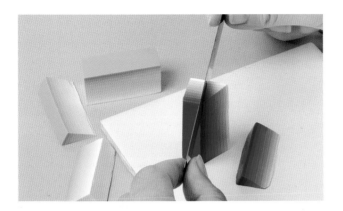

Compress the cane, folding over any edges that stick out, as they will form curved elements that are lovely when repeated. Choose a point of the triangle and use your fingers in a pinching motion to refine the point and press down against the work surface to flatten the opposite side to form it into an equilateral triangle. Turn the cane and continue to refine. Reduce the cane so each of its sides is ½ inch (13mm). Refer to Technique: Elongating a Block on page 83 for tips on reducing canes. Cut off the distorted ends of the cane, as they will not mirror well.

3. To create a master cane that will be recombined into many tessellated or mirrored canes, combine the wedges, making sure they remain straight throughout the cane. Work toward a form that loosely resembles a triangle.

| CREATING TESSELLATED VARIATIONS |

Each of the six variations of tessellated beads shown in Judy's project requires segments from the master cane. While you may not have enough of the master cane to create all of the combinations, if you combine the pieces gently, you can take them apart and try different combinations. Build at least three variations of the tessellated design to add interest to your finished necklace. These examples are but a few of the hundreds that can be built.

1. white center point For the second design, still using 6 segments, look at the side of one of the triangles mirrored in the first cane. Choose a different side to mirror and piece these segments together as you did before, paying close attention to the center point to ensure that the new pattern is different.

2. blue center point This design also uses 6 segments, mirroring the side of the triangle that is different from the first two variations. Piece these segments together as you did before, paying close attention to mirroring the blue point of the triangle in the center.

3. complex For an even more complex pattern, cut two 3-inch- (7.5cm-) long segments from the master cane, mirror one side of the triangles, and re-form them into a new triangle. (Use the technique in step 3 to form the new equilateral triangle.) Stretch and reduce the triangular cane so that each side is ½ inch (13mm) wide. Cut the cane into six 1-inch- (2.5cm-) long segments, and mirror again as in the first three variations. This complex cane can be done in many variations, depending on which sides of the master triangle you chose to mirror for the first part of the step. The image shows only two of these variations.

4. square The master cane can also be recombined into tessellated square canes. Cut two 3-inch- (7.5cm-) long segments of the master cane, and mirror one side of the triangles. Re-form this new, diamond-shaped cane into a square cane by pressing with your fingers and rolling each side with an acrylic rod. Stretch and reduce the square cane so that each side is ½ inch (13mm) wide. Cut the new square cane into 4 equal segments. Mirror these segments so that the centers meet and all sides mirror one another to form the tessellated square cane.

1

2

3

4

4. Tessellating the master cane is the most fun part of the process! For the first design, cut six 1-inch- (2.5cm-) long segments from the master cane. Put 2 triangles together so the sides mirror each other. Repeat, mirroring the same 2 sides, for the other 4 segments. Piece these 3 new segments together so the centers meet and all sides mirror to form a hexagonal cane.

TEMPLATES

1. To make a two-sided twirling bead you need to create a template. Roll out a sheet of scrap polymer to a medium setting. Cut this sheet in half and stack the two halves. Cut the layered sheet into sixteen 1 x 1–inch (2.5 x 2.5cm) square sections. Place each square onto a ceramic tile, and then press until they stick to ensure they remain flat.

Using various plunger-style cutters, cut differently sized and shaped holes into each of the 16 squares.
TIP: Pull the cutter straight up and leave the cut-out section of polymer in place. The outside edge of the internal shape will remain true and will easily pop out after baking.

Place the tile in the oven and cure according to manufacturer's instructions; allow the polymer to cool to room temperature, and then remove each piece from the tile. Each template will be slightly indented, so lay a sheet of 220-grit sandpaper on a flat surface and sand flat.

2. Lay each cured template on a small piece of copy paper and trace the perimeter of the cut-out shape. Fold the paper

in half and lay it down, matching the drawn line with the cut-out shape in the template. Lay a piece of painter's tape along the folded edge of the paper and wrap around the edges of the template. This will act as a guide for the drill bit and ensure you drill exactly on center, which is necessary for the spinning effect. Repeat for each template.

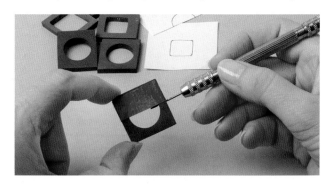

Drill a hole into each template using a #70 drill bit fitted to a variable-speed or hand drill, first through the top and then through the bottom.
TIP: Keep the templates once you're finished with this project, as they can be reused.

TWIRLING BEADS

1. Gather and cut all of your canes into ¹⁄₄-inch- (6mm-) thick slices. Some of the tessellated canes may need to be rounded and reduced to fit the shape of the cutout in the template. Cut out shapes in the striped and checkerboard canes using the cutters that correspond with the openings you cut out of the templates in step 1 of Tessellated Master Cane Templates.

2. Using a paintbrush and a generous amount of repel gel, coat the inside edge of the hole in each template. The repel gel is what allows the center beads to release from the template; otherwise they would bond to the cured template and stay in place permanently. Place a headpin through the drilled holes. Place a slice of black-and-white cane on one side of the opening and a slice of a colored cane on the other, covering the headpin. Press the slices firmly to be sure the cane fully fills the opening. Holding a stiff blade flat against the surface of the template, gently slice off the excess cane on both sides. Repeat for each bead, making sure to create different combinations of black and white and color. With the headpins still intact, place the beads onto a copy paper–covered ceramic tile and cure following the manufacturer's instructions. Allow the beads to cool, remove the headpins, and pop the center beads out.

   TIP: Kato Polyclay can be shiny when cured. You can matte the surface of the polymer by brushing each bead with cornstarch before curing.

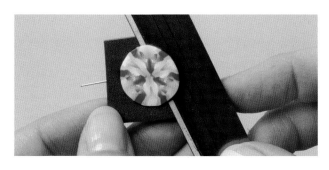

3. To add interest and finish the edges of the twirling beads, add a strip of stripes. Cut 4 to 6 slices of a thin-striped black-and-white cane. Lay the slices down onto your work surface so they butt up right next to each other. Using a sheet of uncoated deli paper, press the slices together so they become one sheet. Lift the sheet from the table, and then line it up so the stripes are perpendicular to the rollers on the pasta machine. Roll the sheet through on the thickest setting. Continue to thin the sheet until you reach the next-to-thinnest setting on the pasta machine. Lightly coat the outside edge of each twirling bead with liquid polymer. Cut a thin strip of the striped sheet, just wide enough to cover the edge of the bead. Wrap the strip around the bead and trim the excess. Replace the headpin to repierce the hole. Repeat for each bead and cure again.

FRAMING BEADS

1. Framing beads house the twirling beads, giving them a place to play and spin. Create a 6 x 8–inch (15 x 20.5cm) sheet of black polymer rolled on a medium setting and cut into 2 x 2–inch (5 x 5cm) squares. Cut ¼-inch- (6mm-) thick slices from the gradated canes (described in step 1 of Technique: Creating Tessellated Canes on page 141) and from the black-and-white canes (described in steps 1–4 of Striped and Checkerboard Canes on pages 139–140).

   Combine the segments of black clay with various black-and-white cane slices to create 12 sections of polymer that are 2 x 2 inches (5 x 5cm), or larger if the cutters you chose for making the framing beads are larger. Combine slices of the green gradated cane with the remaining black-and-white cane slices and repeat with the slices of the turquoise gradated cane to form an additional 12 sections for the reverse side of the framing bead.

   Use uncoated deli paper to adhere the slices together. Apply texture if you'd like; I used Clay Yo Texture Sponges.

2. Lay out the black/black-and-white sections and place a section of color combination alongside each one. Play with the layout of patterns and colors to be sure you like the

order they are placed in on each side. Keep in mind that this necklace can be worn all black and white, a turquoise/green combination—or a bit of both! When you are pleased with your layout, press the two sections together by retexturing each side, creating 12 different two-sided sections. Choose the size and shape of the nesting cutter you plan to use for each of the sections. Vary the sizes and shapes as you decide placement. Remember that smaller beads will be more comfortable at the back of the neck. Using the nesting cutters, press firmly and straight down to cut the outside of the framing bead.

TIP: Most nesting cutters have a seam that creates a bump in the polymer; carefully trim off this bump with a craft knife.

3. Decide which twirling beads you want to place inside each framing bead. Experiment with the patterns, colors, and shapes until you find an arrangement that pleases you. Use the plunger-style cutters that are slightly larger than the twirling bead to cut holes in the framing bead. Place the framing beads onto a paper-covered ceramic tile and cure. If, after these frames are cured and cooled, you find that the holes are not large enough to accommodate the twirling bead, enlarge the hole using sandpaper attached to a craft stick or dowel rod with double-sided tape. Using the same method from step 2 of Tessellated Master Cane Templates on page 140, drill each frame.

NOTE: If you have chosen to use a framing bead for the toggle ring, drill only one hole in that frame.

TWIRLING NECKLACE

1. You may choose to finish your necklace with a purchased clasp, or, as I have done here, use one of the framing beads for a toggle ring. Using wire cutters, cut a suitable length of flexible beading wire. String a crimp bead, the framing bead that serves as the toggle ring, and 1 glass bead. Loop the wire back through the hole in the toggle ring and through the crimp bead, skipping the glass bead, as it acts as a stop for the wire. Using crimping pliers, crimp the crimp bead. For instructions on crimping with crimping pliers, see step 8 in Folded Beads on page 62.

    String the rest of the twirling beads and framing beads onto the wire, placing a rubber O-ring (as shown in the finished image on page 137) or other bead of your choice between each framing bead.

2. To create the toggle bar and decorative spacing beads, form a 2-inch- (5cm-) long snake of scrap polymer, and wrap with a slice from a striped cane. Smooth and roll to close the seam.

3. Cut four 1/8-inch (3mm) segments for decorative, striped ball spacing beads. The number of spacing beads needed for your clasp will depend on the size of the framing bead you choose for the toggle. The beads are strung along with the toggle bar on one end of the necklace and help the toggle bar have the slack needed to pass through the toggle ring.

4. Work the stripes to the top and bottom of the slice so that they meet in the middle and form round, striped beads. Smooth the seams, and roll between your palms to ensure the bead is round.

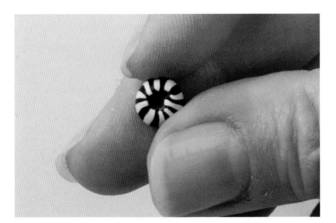

5. Work the stripes to the middle of the ends of the remaining section of wrapped cane, forming nicely rounded ends for the toggle bar. Cure the components following the manufacturer's instructions. Using a #70 drill bit, drill a hole in the center of the toggle bar and each round bead.

6. To finish the necklace, string as many of the small striped beads as necessary, placing O-rings between them, a crimp bead, the toggle bar, and a small glass bead. Loop back through the hole in the toggle bar, and the crimp bead. Using crimping pliers, crimp the crimp bead. Using wire cutters, trim the excess wire on each end.

Exploring movement in jewelry, Judy created an entire line of kinetic jewelry in vibrant jewel tones that invite the wearer to play. This one is appropriately titled *Fidget.*

Cabinet of Curiosities!

Each member of the team had made work that represented movement—Judy, with her kinetic, wholesale line of jewelry; Julie, who uses metal and cold connections to add movement to her pieces; and Wendy, whose pieces occasionally look like they are poised to wriggle away.

Before meeting in the Outer Banks, their planning for the project was minimal—essentially a string of spirited e-mails—but they did establish that the collaboration would take shape around two goals: The finished piece would be table or wall art rather than jewelry, and it would be infused with a sense of movement and energy. Each artist looked at the challenge more as a diversion rather than an assignment—taking seriously the growth opportunity, yet hoping to impart the joy they felt being given the chance to explore together.

Organizing an Embarrassment of Riches

The different design approaches embraced by each artist were clearly demonstrated by what they arrived with at the beach home: Julie with hastily sketched drawings on an airplane napkin; Wendy with a beautifully embellished sketchbook containing numerous notes and fine drawings; and Judy with numerous unfinished samples, which she hastily unpacked while talking and making gestures with her hands. Some of the ideas were quickly discarded, sometimes sheepishly, in the hopes that no one would be offended by the decision; others were completely embraced with loud whoops of joy. Mixing in various ideas from each of their designs, a picture began to appear.

The fun started when they gathered in Julie's room and dumped, right in the middle of her bed, all of the items they had collected while scouring the aisles of hardware, antique, thrift, and craft stores. It was an incredible display of ephemera—metal tubing, 16-gauge wire, small hinges, threaded rods, nuts, bolts, washers, cotter pins, ball chain,

nails, screws, wing nuts, eye bolts, springs, a pulley, metal flashing, antique metal balls and spokes, and so forth. Wendy was particularly drawn to several brightly colored thin springy bracelets that Judy had brought, already envisioning the playful "dance" they could create.

Ideas flowed freely at this point—perhaps too much so. Julie, Wendy, and Judy were having fun brainstorming, but Julie knew they needed to shift into an edit mode. After admiring the items, they began to place only their favorite components on a tray.

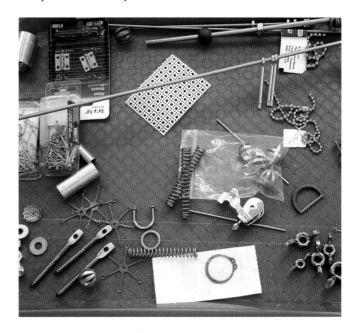

During the initial design phase, Julie, Wendy, and Judy selected their favorite components—the ones that would make the perfect "skeletons," to be embellished with polymer, that would facilitate movement in the piece.

Containing the Creation

At times the group's enthusiasm moved the project along more quickly than perhaps it should have. They had arranged to have a discussion with Jeff about their plans, but when they realized that their creation needed some kind of framework, they immediately ran out of the house in search of a suitable structure, leaving Jeff to wonder where the team had gone. This trip to a local store provided the perfect container: an inexpensive paint set. The paints were hastily set aside—the wooden box itself was the prized item. It was just the thing to contain the moving pieces that Julie, Wendy, and Judy planned to make.

The paint originally stored within the box turned out to be useful, though, as Wendy applied her illustration talents and decorated the box. She chose black and white paints—both to visually anchor the various pieces of metal and polymer that would be attached to the box as well as to mimic the checkerboard canework that Judy planned to use for some of her sculptural elements.

Embracing Independence

Julie, Wendy, and Judy settled into their workstations near the front of the house in a lovely bay window overlooking the marshes and Currituck Sound. From the outset, the project was conceived to allow each of the three team members to work somewhat independently. This approach was in part dictated by Judy's dual role in the retreat—both as author/organizer and as partner for this project. Julie and Wendy good-naturedly embraced Judy's erratic participation, laughingly referring to her contributions as "drive-by art."

Julie, Wendy, and Judy started creating an array of little kinetic sculptures. These elements had a harmonious palette—as Judy's and Wendy's bright polymer hues were softened a bit by stolen pinches from Julie's workspace, and vice versa. Literally, "mix it up" became the mantra as the group gathered several times to evaluate the pieces they had made and to determine if their color choices were harmonious. Some strident black-and-white pieces were subdued with dots or edges of more muted colors.

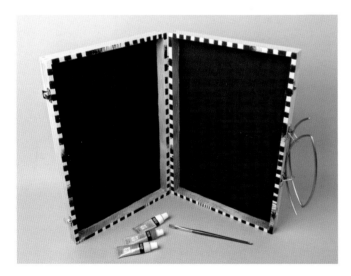

ABOVE: At first, the team thought the structure would sit on a table. But once they realized that hanging it on the wall would provide more opportunities for dangling movement, they created a more interesting hanger so it could mount on the wall. **RIGHT:** Wendy put her graphic-design skills to work adding complementary artwork to the box.

Focusing on Mechanics

The team set to work, figuring out how to create the movement they desired. Their plan was to incorporate the metal components with polymer and then attach them to the box. The question was *how*? Some of the hardware finds—like the pulley—presented the obvious potential for movement. Other pieces required more thought.

The team soon faced a dilemma—how to marry a nonporous item with polymer. But they saw this obstacle as a wonderful challenge. They kept a colorful ceramic bowl in the center of the table to place pieces that they loved but were struggling with. As the week went on, they conferred with others on how best to resolve the issue and came up with a number of brilliant solutions.

Rather than simply pushing springs into polymer, Judy realized that twisting the coils helped to embed them in the polymer, creating a more solid connection between the two materials. In addition, texturing the back of the polymer before applying two-part epoxy helped create a firm bond between the polymer and the wood.

Wendy, excited to use the thin metal spring bracelets that she coveted, chose them to give her polymer legs real bounce and swing. She embedded the springs in the legs prior to curing and attached them to the box by drilling holes slightly smaller than the springs, adding drops of glue, and twisting the legs into position. This technique facilitated the series of "running" legs that eventually adorned the lower half of the box.

ABOVE LEFT: Julie loved that Judy and Wendy were willing to "just let it happen." For her, arriving at the beach almost completely unprepared with just a vague goal did not feel stressful, but rather incredibly liberating.
ABOVE RIGHT: Adding a solid polymer base to each coil made it easy to attach it to the wooden box.

"Our cabinet piece entertains and satisfies me on a visual, functional, and visceral level. I now have new, alternative ways to look at metalworking and making connections."
—*Wendy*

From the beginning, Julie, Wendy, and Judy had known they wanted a crankshaft—something that could be turned to feature dangling elements that would move up and down. Julie used flat-nose pliers to bend 16-gauge plastic-coated wire into a shape that resembled dentil molding. Wendy discovered that the loops or holes on cotter pins and eyebolts threaded easily onto the crank, so they were distributed to whoever wanted to add an embellishment to the crankshaft. Leslie was inspired and quickly offered her donation—a dancing pig.

Once the sculptures had been assembled, Julie added screw-eye hooks (large enough to accommodate the 16-gauge wire) into the sides of the box. She then positioned the crank in the box, bending one end to be a handle and trimming the other closely to the box edge. Wendy finished the ends with decorated pods that were cured, according to manufacturer's instructions, drilled using a $^3/_{16}$-inch (5mm) drill bit, and glued to the wire ends.

"Take two distinctly different artists (Julie and Wendy), catalyze with Judy, and stand back! This dynamic trio set a whirlwind in motion that swept in nearly every other artist. In many ways their piece is the embodiment of the playful collaborations of the week at the beach."

—*Jeff*

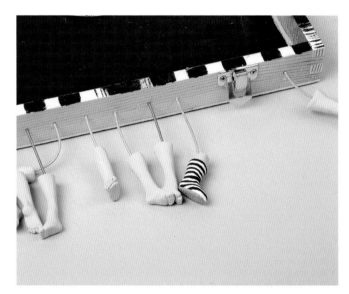

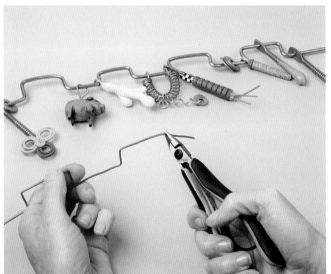

ABOVE LEFT: Jeff offered Wendy a stash of brightly colored nail polish (which he uses to embellish the pins of his own work) to adorn the toenails of the legs, but the group ran out of time to implement this clever idea.
LEFT: Julie kept the ends of the crankshaft straight until the piece could be mounted to the box. This allowed the wire to be threaded through the eye of the screw and kept the crankshaft level.

Adding Playful Elements

Having been officially invited to add their own pieces of "drive-by art," others decided to join in the fun: Robert added metalwork connections; Sarah added a trio of beads that swirled around a dangle; Dayle added a decorated spinner; and Cynthia added her new beach glass for the bead bar. The project was officially open to all!

Judy created striped polymer balls with muted embellishments to use as finials. Julie cut 16-gauge plastic-coated wire, forming it into a hanger at the top of the box. The balls were cured, drilled, and glued to the ends of the wire.

No one on the team was familiar with the threaded brass pieces that Judy had purchased—nor did they even know what they were. Robert solved the mystery with a laugh: They were brass router base inserts. Wendy instantly recognized that they could be repurposed into interesting elements. She filled a bottom piece with a polymer sea scene, and Robert created a lens that he affixed with two-part epoxy into the top piece. (See Technique: Forming a Domed Piece of Plastic on page 108 to create your own plastic lens.) Wendy used the epoxy to attach the bottom insert to the box; when the top piece was screwed on, the lens magnified the art underneath.

Using a jeweler's saw, Julie cut a piece of decorative metal designed to cover vents into a circle. She then backed the metal piece with polymer and riveted metal and polymer

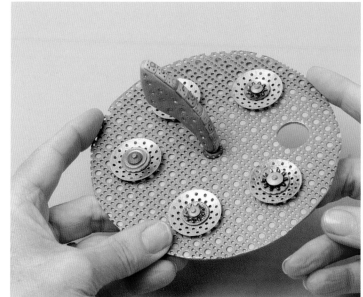

ABOVE: Marrying metal, a nonporous material, with polymer was easy for the handle, as the wire had a plastic coating. Judy used cyanoacrylate, commonly known as Super Glue, as it bonds both types of plastic beautifully. **FAR RIGHT:** Wendy's delight with the thin metal spring bracelets recurs several times in the cabinet. Here they rise from the metal tube almost like branches swaying in the wind. **RIGHT:** Wendy was inspired when she realized that brass router base inserts could be screwed together, allowing them to house a small treasure.

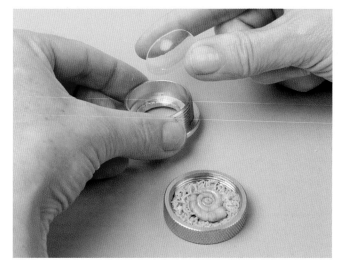

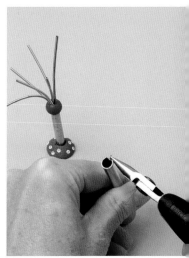

accents in place. (For instructions on riveting see step 7 in Tubular Totems on page 129.) Julie crafted a handle from polymer, embedding a bolt head in the bottom before curing the piece. She then threaded several washers onto the bolt; these lifted the disk off the back of the box, allowing it to spin freely.

Wendy used metal tubing to give height to a fun polymer sprig. Using shears, she made two small cuts in the tubing and then bent the clipped section outward, creating a flap. This flap provided a grip for the polymer on the otherwise slick metal surface.

Thanks to Robert, micro bolts and nuts were aplenty on the team's table. As with the balls shown on the top of the frame, an entire "contraption" could be held to the side of the box simply by embedding a micro bolt into one end of a polymer ball and adding a U-shaped wire into the other end

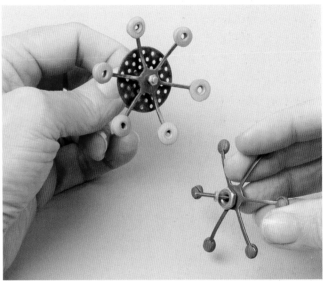

OPPOSITE: Julie left a "viewing" hole in the disk, so when it is spun you can read letters that spell out the team's motto for the week: Running with Scissors!

ABOVE: Micro fasteners were used to connect many of the items to the box. The bolts easily embed into raw polymer, becoming secure when the piece was cured.

ABOVE RIGHT: While visually simple, Julie's spinning spokes were by far the thing that others in the house chose to play with first.

RIGHT: Wendy continued to use those thin, springy bracelets—this time to add an unusual movement to her subverted sea-like creations.

"Making our collaboration was like building a house of cards. A few of the cards fell during the process (amid hoots of laughter and a bad word here or there). We were holding our collective breath as we added the final card; then we exhaled with delight when our house stood on its own."

—*Julie*

before curing. Though complex, the entire sculptural piece is deceptively light, as Wendy created the dangling rings and pod using Sculpey UltraLight after being inspired by the shapes and forms that Sarah and Dayle were creating (see page 69).

Julie's prized items from the tray were vintage brass spokes that she purchased in an antique store. She embellished them with polymer, and stacked them with copper sink screens and nuts. The pieces were threaded onto small thin bolts, and, as with the spinning disk, extra washers were added to create lift and to facilitate movement. She bolted both pieces to the box.

Wendy threaded a chain through a pulley, decorating the ends with pre-cured polymer pieces that resemble the forms she created for her *Subverted Bracelet* (see page 131). She fashioned a base from hammered metal, which she then nailed to the box. By the week's end, everyone in the house delighted in playing with the *Cabinet of Curiosities*, but which of the women would take home the prize? They agreed it would be treated as a time-share and visit each home over the years to come.

"The way the piece came together strengthened my feeling that allowing others to participate in my work—adding elements of their own, suggesting new and better ways to do things, even gently critiquing my contributions—can make me a better artist. My only regret is that readers can't reach right into the pages of this book and play with this piece. It is a joy!"
—Judy

ABOVE: Judy embellished several orphan router bases with her signature striped and checkerboard cane slices. She then added the trimmed pencils and paintbrush, symbolizing Wendy's drawing and painting contributions and providing a great tactile addition.

WHERE TO GO FROM HERE

After reading this book, you may ask yourself how to move forward. The eleven artists who are featured in this book have all been inspired by—and, in turn, influenced—other artists. The six images shown on pages 153–155 only just begin to show the range of influences at play with these eleven artists. No matter how far along you may be on your personal artistic path, inspiration is sure to flow—in one direction or another.

Many of the artists presented in this book are instructors, and they always try to impart to their students to "make the work your own"—a difficult thing to do. There is the need to replicate the lessons to improve your skill, but at some point your voice must begin to be present in your work.

You have taken this journey with us. Now create your own journey! Find an artist in your area who works in polymer (or even another medium) and work on a piece together. Plan a meeting where you bring your own work and discuss what is most important to you about the piece and why. Work together *and* spend time apart to think about the piece and bring new and fresh ideas that push your design and your ability.

Search the Internet for a person or group that excites you. Collaborations can be done long distance! Start a piece, perhaps a focal bead, and send it on to another artist who might add supporting beads or maybe wirework. A third person could join all the pieces together. Each artist adds his or her vision, usually in surprising ways.

Join or host a swap—where a group of artists all make a set number of pieces of work centered around a theme. All the work is gathered by the person hosting the swap, and one piece of each of the other artists' work is then returned to each of the participants. Evaluate how each of the artists interpreted the theme.

Attend everything you are financially able to. Find polymer and art conferences and retreats. Allow yourself to be immersed in those around you and what they are creating. Take note of artwork you see and query the artist who made it: What inspired them? Why did they choose certain colors? How did they solve problems they incurred while creating the piece? Ask them to discuss your work: How would they have done it differently? What might they have added or taken away to make the piece more successful? Making the effort to engage in a broad range of dialogues is bound to stretch and improve your work. Enjoy the journey!

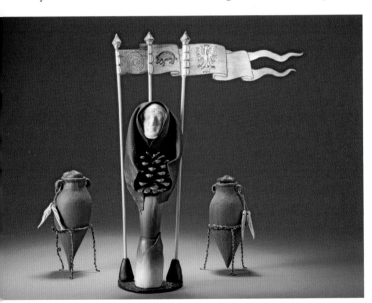

Margaret Reid, *Sylvan*, 2007; polymer, wire, paper, skewers, and pine cone; dimensions variable. Photograph by Laurence Winram. This piece was created during a weeklong workshop in France with Dayle and was inspired by the title of the course: "Discovering Ancient France." Margaret, a colleague and friend of Dayle Doroshow, is always thinking about how to do things differently. Dayle admires the cleanness of her art, the sense of adventure, and that she works with intention.

Karen Woods, *Out of Africa*, 2006; polymer; 13 x 18 inches (33 x 46cm). Photograph by Karen Woods. Karen's prizewinning necklace was inspired by African mudcloth that she was making at the time. Taking a cue from Sarah, whom she considers one of the premier caners in the polymer community, gave her the opportunity to work with complex caning—the technique that makes her heart sing. With a background in textiles and basket weaving, Karen shares an affinity with Sarah Shriver for all sorts of repeat patterns.

RIGHT: When Leslie Blackford looks at a piece that Scott has made, she is immediately transformed into a land of wonder. His work is so oddly unique and simply beautiful. Scott Radke, *Deer Series*, 2005; mixed media; each 13 x 13 inches (33 x 33cm). Photograph by Scott Radke

BELOW: Ron Lehockey, *Hearts*, 2011; polymer; dimensions variable. Photograph by Ron Lehockey. Ron is a general pediatrician in Louisville, Kentucky, who treats children with special challenges. In 2011 he reached seventeen thousand hearts. Ron takes several workshops each year. The techniques that he masters are quickly fashioned into his signature heart pins, donating all of the proceeds to a children's charity. In looking at a pile of pins you can spot ones inspired by Jeff Dever, Sarah Shriver, Judy Belcher, and Lindly Haunani.

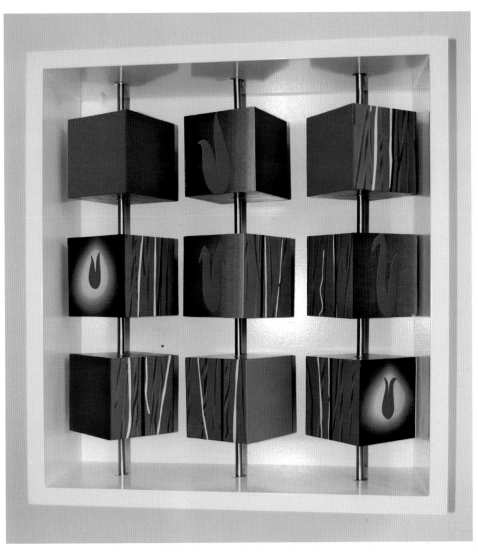

ABOVE: Alev Gozonar, *Tulips*, 2010; polymer, Plexiglas, metal, and wood; 24 x 24 inches (60 x 60cm). Photograph by Alev Gozonar *Tulips* is part of Alev's cube collection, in which the cubes, turning on their own axes, have separate images on each side. The viewer is able to pick the images on the cubes and, therefore, is an active participant in the creative process. Judy Belcher is intrigued by the movement in Alev's work, but more important, the active participation by the public that it inspires. As an art form, polymer has the potential of moving into public spaces—it's something that Alev has mastered in her home country of Turkey.

LEFT: Rachel is one of the few polymer artists who has developed a entire body of work exploring screen printing. Seth Lee Savarick has long admired Rachel's complex surface designs. Rachel Carren, *Hokusai Cupola Brooch*, 2010; polymer and acrylic pigment; 2⅜ x 2⅜ x ⅜ inches (6 x 6 x 1cm). Photograph by Hap Sakwa. Rachel's brooch design is based on the idea of an architectural dome. Color scheme and patterning is after the work of the Japanese artist Katsushika Hokusai (1760–1849).

RESOURCES

Each company is listed with highlights of products they offer, but this is by no means a comprehensive listing. Manufacturers will gladly offer you a listing of companies who sell their products. The other resources listed sell directly. Each artist in this book has a business where they either sell products or artwork or teach classes. Visit their individual websites for more information. In addition, for further inspiration and information about ideas presented in this book, check: www.polymermasterclass.com.

MANUFACTURERS

Polyform Products
1901 Estes Avenue
Elk Grove Village, IL 60007
847-427-0020
www.sculpey.com
Premo! Sculpey, Sculpey III, Sculpey
UltraLight, polymer tools

Staedtler
Staedtler Mars Limited
5725 McLaughlin Road
Mississauga, Ontario L5R 3K5
www.fimo.com
Fimo Classic, Fimo Soft,
polymer tools

Van Aken International
9157 Rochester Court
P.O. Box 1680
Rancho Cucamonga, CA 91729
www.katopolyclay.com
Kato Polyclay, polymer tools

Viva Decor
495 East Erie Avenue
Philadelphia, PA 19134
215-634-2235
www.viva-decor.us
Pardo Art Clay, Pardo
Jewellery Clay

Ranger Industries, Inc.
15 Park Road
Tinton Falls, NJ 07724
732-389-3535
www.rangerink.com
Embossing powders, inks

RETAIL/WHOLESALE SUPPLIERS

Cracker Dog Design—Robert Dancik
203-751-2531
www.fauxbone.com
Faux Bone, saw blades, micro
fasteners, metal tools

Crafted Findings/Metal Clay Findings
49 Hurdis Street
North Providence, RI 02904
888-999-6404
www.metalclayfindings.com
Riveting tool, rivets, eyelets, jewelry
findings

Fire Mountain Gems and Beads
One Fire Mountain Way
Grants Pass, OR 97526
800-423-2319
www.firemountaingems.com
Metalsmithing tools and supplies,
jewelry-making tools and supplies,
adhesive sheets

Polymer Clay Express
9890 Main Street
Damascus, MD 20872
800-844-0138
www.polymerclayexpress.com
All brands of polymers,
polymer tools

Prairie Craft Company
P.O. Box 209
Florissant, CO 80816
800-799-0615
www.prairiecraft.com
Kato Polyclay, Kato tools and videos

Polymer Art Archives
www.polymerartarchive.com

ARTISTS

Judy Belcher
St. Albans, WV
www.judybelcherdesigns.com

Leslie Blackford
Munfordville, KY
www.moodywoods.com

Robert Dancik
Oxford, CT
www.fauxbone.com

Dayle Doroshow
Fort Bragg, CA
www.dayledoroshow.com

Lindly Haunani
Cabin John, MD
www.lindlyhaunani.com

Tamara Honaman
Collegeville, PA
www.thonaman.com

Wendy Wallin Malinow
Portland, OR
www.wendywallinmalinow.com

Sandra McCaw
Westborough, MA
www.sandramccaw.com

Julie Picarello
El Dorado, CA
www.yhdesigns.com

Seth Lee Savarick
Los Angeles, CA
www.slsavarickstudio.com

Sarah Shriver
San Rafael, CA
www.sarahshriver.com

Cynthia Tinapple
Worthington, OH
www.polymerclaydaily.com

BIBLIOGRAPHY

Belcher, Judy. *Polymer Clay Creative Traditions: Techniques and Projects Inspired by the Fine and Decorative Arts.* New York: Watson-Guptill Publications, 2006.

Dancik, Robert. *Amulets and Talismans: Simple Techniques for Creating Meaningful Jewelry.* Cincinnati, OH: North Light Books, 2009.

Haunani, Lindly and Maggie Maggio. *Polymer Clay Color Inspirations: Techniques and Jewelry Projects for Creating Successful Palettes.* New York: Potter Craft, 2009.

Haunani, Lindly and Pierrette Brown Ashcroft. *Artists at Work: Polymer Clay Comes of Age.* Gaithersburg, MD: Flower Valley Press, 1997.

Picarello, Julie. *Patterns in Polymer: Imprint and Accent Bead Techniques.* Waukesha, WI: Kalmbach Books, 2011.

Roche, Nan. *The New Clay: Techniques and Approaches to Jewelry Making.* Gaithersburg, MD: Flower Valley Press, 1992.

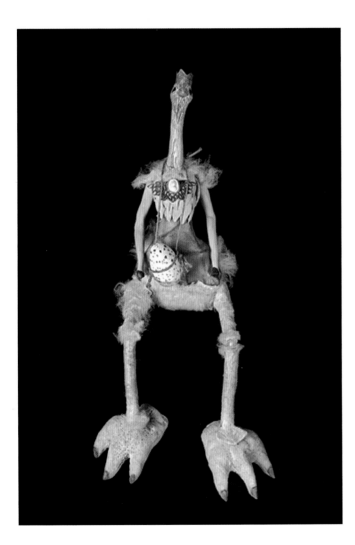

"One autumn I took a class with Robert at Arrowmont School of Arts and Crafts in Gatlinburg, Tennessee. He piled personally made artifacts on his desk, and I immediately chose a three-dimensional piece made from wire. Without hesitating, he gave me permission to use it. As I worked on my vision that week, Robert shared thoughts and help. Ophelia is the result of a natural collaboration, unplanned and inspired."

—*Leslie*

Leslie Blackford and Robert Dancik, *Ophelia and the Egg*, 2010; polymer, wire, copper, nylon, hemp, antique cameo, glass beads, and marbles; 11 x 3 x 2 inches (28 x 7.5 x 5cm). Photograph by Leslie Blackford

ABOUT THE AUTHORS

JUDY BELCHER is the author of *Polymer Clay Creative Traditions* and coauthor of several other books. She teaches workshops and speaks around the country and internationally, sharing her fascination with polymer. She has organized international conferences, developed programs for arts organizations, and demonstrated at galleries, trade shows, and on television. Her work has been in national exhibits and is sold in retail galleries around the country. Judy's home and studio are in West Virginia, a state whose commitment to its artisans is unrivaled.

TAMARA HONAMAN teaches and speaks about jewelry making internationally. She also contributes jewelry-making projects, articles, and designs to magazines, books, television programs, and Fire Mountain Gems and Beads, who produced her full-length DVD, *Secrets to Art Clay Success*. She is the founding editor of *Step-by-Step Beads*; former editor of *Step-by-Step Wire* and "Step-by-Step" in *Lapidary Journal Jewelry Artist*. Tamara lives and works in Pennsylvania as a jewelry designer.

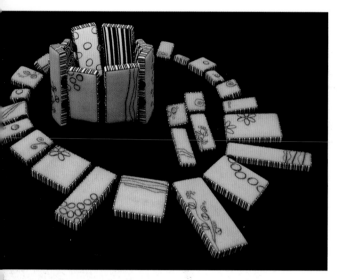

ABOVE: Judy Belcher, *Wearing Joy*, 2010; polymer and sterling silver; dimensions variable. Photographs by Judy Belcher

RIGHT: The canework of the necklace, bracelet, and earrings shown here was formed to mimic the patterns in the jacket. "Fiber artist Kerr Grabowski and I collaborated to create this ensemble for the Synergy2 exhibit. Kerr created the handpainted silk crepe and chiffon jacket, modeled here by Maria Belcher; I created the corresponding jewelry." —Judy

OPPOSITE LEFT: Tamara Honaman, *Layers*, 2011; ¼ x 1¾ inches (8mm x 4.5cm); metal clay, fine silver, and wire. Photograph by Richard K. Honaman Jr.

OPPOSITE RIGHT: Jeff Dever, *Sheltered Effusion*, 2010. 7 x 5¾ x 16¼ inches (18 x 14.5 x 42cm); polymer, steel wire, and plastic-coated copper wire. Photograph by Jeff Dever. *Sheltered Effusion* is a sculptural basket created for the invitational exhibition "New x 3" at Blue Spiral gallery in Asheville, North Carolina.

ARTISTIC SUPPORT

The lens to our world, the photographer RICHARD K. HONAMAN JR., received his BA from New Jersey Institute of Technology. A Photoshop expert, Richard has published his images of model renderings in various publications, including *Architectural Record*. He lives in Collegeville, Pennsylvania, with his wife, Tamara Honaman, where he supports her career with photography and web design, works full-time as director of technical projects for Signature Information Solutions, LLC, a company of Lexis Nexis, is an officer with the Pennsylvania Freedom of Information Coalition, coach for his son's football team, and is involved in community service as a football league board member.

Our eyes, ears, and consult for the week, JEFFREY LLOYD DEVER received his BFA from Atlantic Union College in 1976. He is founding partner and creative director of Dever Designs and its subsidiary, FreshArt Illustration, in Laurel, Maryland. He was on the contract/ adjunct faculty of Maryland Institute College of Art for twenty years, where he taught illustration and graphic design. Jeffrey's polymer clay vessels and jewelry are represented in numerous museums, galleries, and publications. He enjoys teaching his signature techniques whenever possible.

Jeff's eyes, ears, and consult for the week (and his lovely wife of twenty-six years), KAY ROSBURG graduated magna cum laude in music education and has worked for Dever Designs since 1988. Her duties include the management of the studio, accounts receivable and payable, purchasing, correspondences, and marketing. Her hobbies include participation in her church's hospitality ministry, book club, choir, and handbells group. She and Jeff have two adult children.

Creator of the hearth of our home for the week, personal chef JIM GLASS came to this project with experience in fine-food retail and catering; however, this was his first opportunity as a personal chef. His professional background is in human resources training and development, where he worked in New York and Southern California. Jim holds an MA in organizational psychology from Columbia University and a BA in German studies from Brown University. He is married to Seth Lee Savarick, who was a collaborator in this project.

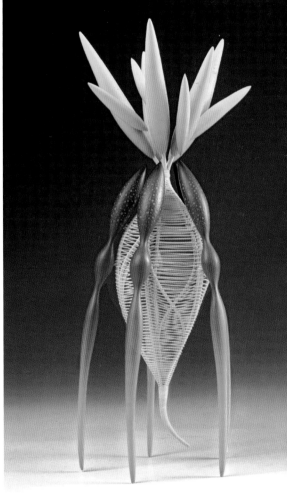

INDEX *note:* page numbers in italics indicate photos and captions